Soul

SUCCESS

SUCCESS

**STORIES AND LESSONS OF FEMALE LEADERS
WHO TURNED PILES OF SH*T INTO
NUGGETS OF GOLD**

MEGAN McCANN

gatekeeper press

Columbus, Ohio

Soul Success: Stories and lessons of female leaders who turned piles of sh*t into nuggets of gold

Published by Gatekeeper Press
2167 Stringtown Rd, Suite 109
Columbus, OH 43123-2989
www.GatekeeperPress.com

The cover design and editorial work for this book are entirely the product of the author. Gatekeeper Press did not participate in and is not responsible for any aspect of these elements.

ISBN (paperback): 9781662900112
eISBN: 9781662900129

Table of Contents

How to Use This Book

You know that feeling you get when you step out of a juicy yoga class or massage? Or when you step into a nice, warm jacuzzi and can't help but let out a deep, long sigh? My wish for you is that this book gives you the same feeling: tools to access your joy and enter into that space where all of the sudden, your worries don't seem as big as you had made them to be.

I firmly believe that the universe is continually sending us messages of growth, love, and understanding. You picked up this book for a reason, and while you might not know what that reason is, I hope you're ready to listen, because it's only then that the magic happens.

The stories you're about to read are from women with different backgrounds, cultures, and perspectives. Some are sailor-mouthed bad asses, some are deep and soulful, but what they all have in common is a commitment to make an impact on this planet and thrive amongst the shit.

Maybe you're going through a rough patch and aren't on top of your game. Know that you're not alone. If you feel that way now, know that you don't have to stay there, sister friend. I know what feeling alone is like. It sucks a big fat one. And I judged the crap out of everyone, especially myself. You don't have to hide in a cave to feel alone. You could be the social chair of your town and still feel like you're the only one who experiences your struggles. I'm here to show you that's a lie. I'm here to be your spiritual matchmaker and introduce you to some badass women who, through story, might just give you permission to reach your next level.

So let's dance, shall we?

I invite you to grab a cup of tea or a glass of wine and read with an open heart. We have much to share with you.

If you're anything like me, your inner critic is loud. You've faced some challenges but there's a fire inside you that knows you're ready to step into your next level. You're ready to let go of the bullshit that has made you play small in the past because it's time, my love. It's time for you to stop giving so much attention to the minutia in your life. It's time for you to take your power back.

Yes, this book is for your enjoyment. It's made for you to feel all the feels. But if you're open, this book is also your permission to play big. I used to hear inspired stories and say to myself, *Yeah, whoop-de-doo! That's great for them,* but a part of me was envious of that inspiration. This is not another *"Hey everyone, look at how great I am!"* kind of book because as you read on, you'll hear about more failures, setbacks, and quirks than you would normally read in a book like this. And you know what the funny thing about that is? Throughout the years, I've come to love those parts about myself (and others for that matter) the most. Perfect is so damn boring. Being flawless is overrated. I'd like to see Maybelline create a "Flaw-full" product line. Yeah, I'd buy that shit today because we all have flaws, baby, and the true beauty comes when we can embrace them. (Cue the wind blowing in my face and blue-steel look, because my eyes are directed right at you, baby!).

Let me give you some more proof to show you how weird and flawed I am: I always seem to get salad stuck in my front teeth. I constantly have boogers in my nose. My size D boobs from high school now more likely resemble deflated size A car tires. Losing my iPhone is a weekly struggle. I can't remember anything unless I've written it down somewhere. I've made some horrible financial investments. I've loved and looked up to people who didn't deserve my trust. When I did my photoshoot for this book, we took 1,300 photos and 1,111 seemed to have my eyes closed. I love corny jokes, fine wine, strong language, pushing boundaries, and at the same time consider myself a soft and spiritual person. I love yoga and I also love gluten. My alter ego is a DJ named "DJ Wiki Wiki Wikipedia" who has the best raps, rhymes, and flow from any white girl from So Cal. I'm an athlete and a hippy. When I dance I think I'm JLO, but my moves are closer to Julia Louis-Dreyfus' performance in Seinfeld. Chewing gum makes me tired. It really grinds my gears when people forget to turn their turn-signal off on the highway. My math brain has completely retired so even simple equations can sometimes make me feel perplexed. Shall I go on?

But I've also accomplished some pretty cool stuff. If I had defined my level of worth based on failures or quirks alone, then the accomplishments you'll read about would never have happened. Instead of putting myself in a box and saying that I'm stupid because my 3rd grade teacher said so, I shifted my focus. I could have given into the lie that I'm not smart because of my SAT score, but then I never would have pursued a Masters Degree from USC and graduated with honors.

Instead of focusing on my failures as weaknesses, I made a decision to focus on the lessons I learned from those failures—and it *is* a decision. Your circumstances don't define who you are, it's what you do about them. My hope is that you understand that your failures are not failures at all. They're love notes from the universe that you're ready to expand.

This book is about you. This book is about putting on your big-girl pants and stepping up, even if you're falling flat on your face with just one pant leg in (in case you're wondering, I've done that more than once). And by the way, if you're a loving man who is ready to expand, this book is for you, too. In fact, I don't have the studies to prove it yet, but I'm fairly certain that reading this book will enhance your sex life.

I recommend grabbing a pen and making a to-do list to pursue that dream you've been putting off. The women you're about to meet will not just tell you about their journeys, they'll also give you action steps you can begin implementing today. If you take them on, I promise you sister friend, you'll experience a shift. It's time, my new friend. Yes, I'm coaching you to stop your whining so you can get to work. Your life depends on it.

So, sit back and relax, but also know that these stories are your permission to go out and pursue the things you've been holding off because of your kids, your husband, the government, the economy, your boss, your parents, your dog, your fish, your plants, your money troubles, or that douchebag of a friend who's told you that you could never do it. The stories of these women are here to inspire you to believe you *can* do it because *they* did it, even amongst the chaos. These women are alchemists, turning their struggles into their greatest gift: piles of shit into nuggets of gold.

My Request Of You

1. **Avoid comparison.** Comparison is the thief of opportunity and expansion. The stories you're about to hear are unique to the storytellers. They're not blueprints for how you should live your life. Fight the urge to think you should have accomplished more by now. That thinking will only hold you back and, quite honestly, it's not true. So please, stop comparing yourself to the women who did it better and faster and without stretch marks. She is likely doing the same with someone else. Honor that you are doing your best and improving every day because, my love, that's enough.

2. **Read with an open heart.** Open your heart to love, forgive, heal, feel the depths of all the feels, and fight judgment. When we judge, we close off the portals of connection, of love, of oneness with spirit. You need these tools of the open heart to invite growth and betterment and the energy that drives us to our highest potential. If a story or situation triggers you in a certain way, I invite you to ask yourself why. When we judge others, it is often because they mirror how we feel about ourselves. That being said, stop judging yourself too 'cause you're bangin' girlfriend! And you need to know that.

3. **Be ready to think outside the box.** Consider how you can implement these tools creatively into your life, career, business, and relationships. There isn't

one roadmap to joy and success. There are multiple ways to get there. You might jump on the turtle's back with a slow and steady pace, or you might hop on the jet and fast-track it to your destination: everything you've ever wanted. What matters are the strides you take to get there.

Introduction: Piles of Shit

I fell asleep on the toilet again. I woke up to my face being held up by my fists, which were being held up by my elbows, resting on my thighs. I talked myself into walking back to bed, with two red elbow marks on my legs. Despite my fatigue, I had to laugh.

Before kids, I would get up only once a night, but now it's more like three or four, mostly to empty my post-childbirth bladder.

I was tired. No, I was beyond tired. I was so exhausted I could barely muster the strength to open one eye. Did you know that dolphins sleep with one eye open and one eye closed? It serves a dual purpose. One reason is it helps them regulate their breath. If both eyes were to close like us, they would suffocate. The second reason is that keeping one eye open is a defense mechanism against predators.

While predators for dolphins consist mainly of sharks, my predator is a 3-year-old human named Galena. After that latest toilet-sleeping episode, I tiptoed back to my bed praying I wouldn't wake her on the other end of the hall. If I woke up my 7-year old, that would suck, but all would be fine because she'd go right back to sleep and start drooling like her mother. But if I woke up Galena, she'd either come into bed and kick me in the head all night, or demand to go downstairs and eat "cheer cheers," aka Cheerios.

There is nothing cheerful about 3am Cheerios.

I crawled back into bed gently so as not to wake my husband. He has suffered from insomnia since a brain injury at 19, so even the slightest tug of our comforter could wake him up for good. Another predator. My house is swimming with them.

As you could see, there's a lot on the line in my house when one goes to the bathroom at night, and it's scary as fuck. As I plopped my head back onto my foam pillow, I thought to myself, *Wow. This is heaven right here.* I was going to sleep so good.

I shut both of my eyes, confident I was clear of my predators and I wouldn't die. As I found myself starting to enter dreamland, I could hear my heart thumping. The thumping seemed like it was getting louder. It didn't take long for me to realize that wasn't my heart, it was the sound of feet.

Fuck.

I can always tell who's coming by the cadence of their feet. My seven-year old, Mykala, has a girl pancake butt and long legs like me so her strides are longer and softer. Galena's butt is juicy and her short legs pound harder, louder, and more frequent. And if you've been around toddlers, you know that they don't walk. Even if the destination is two feet away, they run from point A to point B every single time.

Dolphins can stay awake and swim for up to five days without fatiguing because with the one-eye method, half of their brain is sleeping while the other is awake. As I opened one eye, I couldn't ignore the fact that at that very moment, I wanted to be a dolphin. You know you're tired when you're begging for one-eyed sleep. As I heard the footsteps get louder, I recognized the pattern—frequent, loud, and running.

Double fuck. The killer shark was coming.

When she approached our room, I heard footsteps stop at our door. Did she fall asleep walking? Which animals do that? I held my breath and listened. Maybe she plopped down on the floor and fell asleep. Maybe I could fall back asleep. Even just thirty minutes of sleep would be heaven.

And then I heard it. A fart. One more thing a discerning parent can use to distinguish her children, one from the other. This one was long and loud and sounded like, get ready for it... a faint, broken bagpipe. It was long and sad-sounding, but funny—far more cheerful than 3 am Cheerios. So funny my tired cheeks smiled. And then she farted again.

Longer and louder.

I giggled and snorted out loud, because a bald and chubby three-year old farting is freakin' funny. A few seconds later she walked over to my husband's side of the bed and said, "Dada, I have a poo poo."

Part of me thought, *Hell yes!* she went to Daddy. But I also knew he was as tired as I was, and he wouldn't be able to get back to sleep after she had her way with him. My sweet husband took her so I could sleep, but at this point there was no going back to sleep for me, either. I stayed in bed wide-awake for another half-hour before I cut my losses to relieve my tired husband.

And here I am, typing away, two hours later, watching Disney cartoons downstairs while my hubs rests next to me and Galena sucks her thumb, eyes wide and smiling because she knows she had won. She usually does.

I'm tired as fuck, but not angry. I'm inspired.

I'm not going to lie: I would love a good sleep right now more than anything. But there's also something deep inside of me that's so lit up that even the thumb-sucking, three-year-old shark sitting next to me can't kill. There's something inside of me that's BIG. Lying here on my couch at 37 years of age, typing away with one eye open, I have found what energizes me, feeds me, fuels me.

I do this for her. The thumb-sucking shark sitting next to me. For Galena and Mykala. Two of the causes of me losing my iPhone along with millions of brain cells every day. For my little bagpipe farter and her sister, who's sleeping in her bed dreaming of boys, kids bop, and her upcoming teenage years, which I fear will send me to an early grave.

And I do it for Luc, my twin flame and husband, who has always supported and believed in me. I do it for him, knowing that since the first day we met it was a divine connection. I do it for the man who reminded me that the purest kind of joy and fulfillment comes from the simple things.

They are my why.

My hope with this book, my mission, is guiding the modern-day woman who is overworked and overwhelmed, to find her joy. I've coached a hell of a lot of women over the years and I've never once met one who didn't appear overextended. Not once.

The world requires a lot more out of us today, and we never fail to respond. Yes, it might be messy. No, it's not perfect at all. And it's hard as fuck. But we do it. And we're pretty badass. This is why I felt called to create this project; to celebrate the superwomen across the world, the alchemists who turn shit into gold. Because there are women like me, awake at 3am, and thriving in their own personal shit storm.

They are sitting on their couch nursing their newborn babies. They are up at 3am working the graveyard shift to support their kiddos. They are up caring for their sick husbands, wives, or children. They are up at 3am worrying about their friend who has cancer, or their kid who just went off to college, or their sick dog. Or maybe, just maybe...They are also up at 3am creating, because they're like me; inspired. And maybe just a tad bit tired.

Over the course of the years, I've met the women in this book and I've heard their stories. They have written books, blogs, and podcasts. They have spoken on stages. They have launched businesses, non-profits, and large-scale events to spread their message. I am blessed to say that most of these women have spoken on my stage at The Soul Success Summit. While many have experienced overwhelming situations, the one common theme is that they managed to come out on top. These women embody leadership and have inspired us to the point of tears. You're about to hear stories that will make your heart thump. Stories that will make you laugh, snort, and cry all at the same time. You're about to meet women who have turned piles of shit into nuggets of gold. These are the women of Soul Success®.

Just thinking about these stories, I can actually hear my heart thumping. And no, it's not Galena's feet.

CHAPTER 1

The Event

"The wound is where the light enters you."
- Rumi

There wasn't a dry eye in the room. I held my breath, desperately trying to hold back my tears. As silly as it sounds, crying in front of people always seemed shameful to me. Like if you see me crying, all my deepest secrets will be revealed and you'll find out what a huge sap I am. I'm also an ugly crier. Eyes pulsating, snot everywhere, scrunchy face kind of crier. I'm the Claire Danes of ugly crying. It's deep, dramatic, and un-sexy. By the way, I love you Claire Danes and your ugly crying is beautiful and magical, especially in Romeo and Juliet. However, unlike your ugly crying, mine likely would be banned from movies forever.

Nevertheless, little tears started running down my face.

As the host of my first large-scale event, I scanned the room to witness the reactions of the speaker's story. I knew it was heavy. She had been through a lot. She had likely experienced more trauma in her 35 years of life than all 50 of us in the room combined. When you run an event like this, a million questions run through your head every minute. Was it too much for people to handle? Could they relate to her grief? Would they feel inspired by the end of her talk or hate me because I made them sit for 90 minutes and listen to her speak?

And when you're a perfectionist like me, the questions don't stop until you've found the answer you want to hear.

Everyone crying is a good thing, right? It either means they feel deeply connected to her, or wait, maybe the event is so bad they are crying just thinking about the money they spent to make it to Santa Barbara. They'll want a refund! But I already spent all the money on the venue. I can't do refunds! Maybe Michelle, the venue owner will find pity on me and give me a partial refund on the venue so I can refund everyone their tickets?

These are just some of the kind of crazy thoughts that go through your head when you're a super-empathic event host who also happens to be a Scorpio. Running an event like this can turn you into a raging control freak. You find yourself taking responsibility for your guests' every feeling. It's ludicrous.

Here's a fairly accurate look into my train of thoughts at one point earlier that day…

Why does that girl have a stink face?

Or does she just have really bad gas?

If she does have bad gas, then did I serve her something bad?

But I did provide gluten and dairy free options?

And why is the music delayed?

Awkward silence!

Somebody fix the music now!

I can actually hear the woman on the other end of the room breathing!

No one is talking!

Did I mess this up?

Oh wait, this is the meditation section. Everyone, shhhhhhh.

Why can't I hear the girl next to me breathing?

Is she choking? Oh wait, she's breathing. Thank God!

Everyone seems peaceful in their meditation. This event rocks!

But who the hell is the next speaker? The meditation is almost over.

Fuck, it's me.

The mind is a funny thing, and if you're not careful it will drive you crazy. So, back to the speaker. While she was getting to the unbelievable trauma from her story, all of a sudden, I felt someone tap on my shoulder. It was my friend, Jen, who lives in my hometown in Idaho. Her eyes were red, and she was panting. For some reason I knew that it wasn't from the speaker. There was something else. Little did I know that she was about to deliver me news that would change everything.

"I just got a text from Tyler. He said that his friend Gibby just passed away."

For a brief moment I thought how weird it was that he also had a close friend named Gibby since it was such an unusual name. But then reality sank in and my heart dropped. I couldn't breathe. My husband had been with Gibby just the other night. He was helping Luc watch our girls back in Idaho while I was here in Santa Barbara putting this event together.

I felt paralyzed.

I sat there for about fifteen minutes in silence, motionless. I didn't know what to think or do. It was as if I had entered a different dimension. It was as if the room was spinning and I no longer felt control over anything. I was overwhelmed with emotion, and at the same time I felt incapacitated. If a fly had landed on my shoulder, I probably would have fallen off my chair.

It couldn't be true.

Meanwhile, the entire energy of the room shifted. It was almost as if a dark cloud hovered over me and affected everyone under the same roof. The speaker had gotten to the intense part of her story, talking about the point in which her mother left her for good. The feeling of loss and mortality took over me. Shit was heavy and I couldn't take it anymore. It sent me over the edge. I wept, Claire Danes-style, and felt all eyes in the room lasering in on me, not the speaker. They all thought I was weeping for her but had no idea the truth behind my tears.

I ran out of the room and called my husband. I was so preoccupied by the Summit, I hadn't talked to him in two days. Boy, did I feel like a dick.

What must he be going through? I knew he wasn't going to be okay.

"Hello?" He answered.

"Babe? Are you ok?"

I didn't have to tell him what I was referring to. He knew I knew. And he started bawling.

I had so many questions that I needed answered. I was sweating, confused, and angry. It felt like a dream. I wanted him to tell me that it was an ugly rumor.

"What happened?" I asked. This was probably the last thing he wanted to answer at this point, but I had to know.

"Gib came out to dinner with me and the girls the other night. I asked him to come over and watch movies with us but he said he had to go home and pack because he was leaving early for NYC in the morning. So we dropped him off at his house and he unexpectedly passed that night." Luc was crying like I never heard him cry before. He was a mess. I was surprised he had the energy to pick up the phone.

Two days had gone by and my sweet husband was going through all this grief without me. His pain must have been insurmountable. I have to admit I was a little pissed he didn't tell me. I was a basket case of emotions.

"*Where are the girls*? Are they okay?"

"*Yes, they are fine.*"

"*Do they know?*"

"*Yes. I told them.*"

There I was. Pissed again that he didn't consult me about this. They loved Gibby. To process a death from someone they knew so well and were just eating dinner with, at one and five years old, requires careful thought and consideration. My past life as a school counselor was trying to break through. I tried to imagine the damage this would bring to them, but little did I realize how much Gibby's death would affect my own life in the following year.

"*Why didn't you tell me?*" I cried.

"*I didn't want it to ruin your big weekend. I know how important this is to you.*"

"*Well that's very sweet. But you still should have told me.*"

After a few more minutes of questioning my husband and offering him love, I wiped my tears and went back into the event wondering if it was still going on. I didn't want to go back in, but I had been preparing for this weekend for more than a year. I had envisioned this moment, closing out the event at my first big Summit, countless times, but in a matter of seconds this BIG MOMENT didn't seem to matter anymore.

I channeled every bit of emotional strength I had. My section in the program was next. I needed to pull my shit together. When I entered the room, everyone was laughing and dancing. The energy was high. The speaker had just finished her uplifting and inspiring story. So I joined the group and put on a fake smile. I tried to pretend that nothing happened, but deep down there was an open wound that would need attention soon.

As I went up on stage I could feel the wound scarring my chest. It was heavy. I felt exposed and wondered if everyone in front of me could feel my pain. I don't remember what I said on stage that afternoon. It could have been amazing, or it could have been the worst display of public speaking anyone has ever experienced to this date.

That day led me to reflect on so many different things. The contrast of highs and lows left me weak. But after hearing inspiring stories all weekend, I felt moved, touched, and filled with awe. Gibby's death reminded me that we are mortal. Our time here on earth is precious, and there are so many people in the world who will never tell their story.

"But what if people forget him?" I later asked my husband.

Gibby led multiple lives. He was a businessman and a good one. But he was also a real, live, breathing rock star. He played with Tenacious D under an alias so his business colleagues wouldn't find him on Spotify and hear his song about "super-hot girls who poop on dates." He was a comedian with sophomoric humor who could give you a complete business analysis in a matter of minutes. About a month before he passed, he had just completed his final masterpiece, a beautiful dream home that he designed and built with the help of some good friends, my husband included. He could compete in a triathlon without training after smoking weed the night before. Yeah, he was that dude. And he was hot.

Gibby had lived more in his 41 years than most people live in a lifetime. I didn't want his story to end. It made me sad to think about the reality we mortals face when we see our timely death. People mourn, but eventually they go on with their lives and never really understand the real trials and tribulations that each of us face. People like Gibby live a very full life, but then one day they move onto the nonphysical world and leave the rest of us wondering who that person really was, deep down. I knew Gibby, I saw him every day. He was a best friend to my husband and we shared many incredible memories together. But, did I *really* know him? Did I know his *true* story?

I didn't want people to forget him because if they did, it would signify that our time here is insignificant. This isn't just about Gibby. It's about all of us living a legacy that is remembered and celebrated, even after we pass. It's about our story and the courage it takes to share it.

If I could take a wild hunch, I'd guess that you have a powerful story that's brewing, too. I am confident that we were all brought here on this earth to learn lessons that complete our soul. I haven't met one person who doesn't have at least one story that has the power to move the emotions of others. As a sociologist and counselor, I take the time to listen and understand. When I see a homeless person holding up a sign on the street begging for money, or a drug addict underneath the freeway shouting at the pole, or the speaker on stage who is the CEO of her company and founder of a global non-profit, my first thought is always *What happened to them? What trauma have they faced, and what did they do about it to get where they are right now?*

And here we are, my friend. United in this book through stories of women with lessons to teach us. One question I'd like to ask you is, *What happened in your life that brought you to this moment right here?*

Both homeless and successful people weren't brought into the world that way, just like we weren't brought into the world with scars and self-limiting beliefs. We were brought into this world without words, judgments, failures, or successes. We were brought here naked and pure. But eventually, life circumstances happen, and how we react to those circumstances creates momentum either *toward* or *away* from joy, fulfillment, and connection.

My three sisters and I couldn't be more different. I am loud and have crazy ideas that would never cross their minds. I got into more trouble in high school than any of them. Yep, I was T-R-O-U-B-L-E. I had numerous Minors in Possession of Alcohol (MIP) and a Driving Under the Influence (DUI) by the age of 22. I was voted "Life of the Party" in high school and my grades were just above average. My saving grace was my athletic ability, which was the only reason why I had the slightest amount of confidence.

In contrast, my sisters never got in trouble with the law and partying was not their jam. God bless them. They're all brilliant educators without an entrepreneurial bone in their bodies. I'm the lonely black sheep.

How is it that people brought into the same family with similar circumstances could turn out to be completely different?

This question has always rattled my brain. What's even more fascinating to me is hearing the stories of people who overcome their struggles and prosper. What was it inside of them that told them not to give up? What tools did they access to walk a greater path? I love hearing about what people have had to experience in order to become better versions of themselves. It is through story that we learn, connect, and improve. The person I am today is not just based on my experience, but also largely influenced by what my community of others has taught me through their stories.

I love hearing stories about human flaws. Perfection is over-rated. Hearing these stories from people who overcome obstacles and bounce back from failure can give us the confidence to overcome our own challenges and failures.

The Birth of Soul Success®

On a random day in the fall of 2017, I had a crazy idea to run a large-scale event with a new concept. The thought was from out of nowhere, it felt like it wasn't even mine. I had so many reasons to ignore it. I had a brand-new baby, I was trying to build an online business, I had no proof it would work, I had never done anything like it before, I was maxed out on time, I didn't have much of a platform yet. The list goes on, and every item on the list was reason enough to ignore the idea. But the pull of it was too powerful to ignore. It grew so strong I felt as though I might lose a part of myself if I didn't pursue it.

I had been running small retreats for a few years by then, and though I had directed sizable events for companies, I was nowhere near ready to run a huge event on my own. I was still building my second business as a strategy coach.

I was teaching yoga some days and working with business clients other days. On the surface, it seemed I was working two polar opposite businesses: spirituality and business strategy. This apparent dichotomy is a theme in my life. One half of my soul wants to be uberly successful as a speaker, leader, and innovator. That part of me loves dressing up, fancy parties, and acting on larger-than-life ideas. This side of me gets shit done and expects nothing less than the best.

At the same time, my hippy side wants to live on a remote beach in Costa Rica where I can eat vegan soup, drink homemade kombucha, plan my next Sanskrit tattoo, and practice yoga in my bikini while my kids run on the beach naked. This part of my soul just wants to rest, relax, be present, and enjoy the simple things.

But these two sides only *seem* like a contrast. During yoga classes, I would take principles from the Yoga Sutras of Patanjali to help facilitate a powerful asana and inward discussion during my students' practice. And later in the day, I would work with my business clients. I discovered, soon enough, though, that my private clients needed to hear and understand the same principles in their business lives.

Case in point: the first of the five Niyamas (habits of yoga) is *shaucha*, cleanliness of mind and clearness in speech. I realized that many of my clients were having a difficult time with shaucha in their business, because they still held onto old garbage from previous life experiences. The process of cleansing and decluttering the mind and the body would open up an entirely new portal of speech and purpose in their business. How powerful is that?

These daily encounters, integrating spiritual practices into business concepts, helped me understand how many of us can benefit from the marriage of *Soul* and *Success*. So I reached out to my friend, Alisa, who I had hired initially to help me build a social media presence. She is an excellent public speaker and business powerhouse, and so I told her about my idea.

"What if we created an event together?" I said. "It would be like a business conference and yoga retreat at the same time?"

She looked at me silently for a while. And then simply said, "No."

I couldn't blame her. It did seem like an odd concept.

"But I could teach yoga and meditation. I could help the attendees create 90-day plans and how to build their business with alignment. You could talk about social media and online business systems. It will be the masculine meets the feminine, and we need both if we want to be successful. It will be amazing."

Again.

"No."

"But you could make really good money doing this! And, you'll get more exposure and clients from it."

And finally, she was listening.

That conversation sparked new creativity and gave birth to a part of my soul that has been hungry to come out for years. This was it. We were going to create the best event ever! The event would celebrate women coming together from all walks of life and be exposed to the same mission—that if we want to be successful, we need to lock arms and do it together. This event would change the way women run their businesses. It would change the world! Hell-to-the-yeah!

Between both of our networks, it would sell out in no time. And the name? Ohhhh... wow! Soul Success Summit? Who doesn't love soul? And who doesn't love success? Who doesn't love alliteration? They would come for the name alone.

To say I was excited is an understatement. So we put together a plan and launched it. We posted online, created email campaigns, ad campaigns, and called all our friends. I couldn't wait for the first person to sign up. Who would it be? Soon we'd have to hire security to keep applicants from throwing elbows at each other. This was going to be the best thing since Spanx.

One week later... Crickets.

It's okay, I told myself. People needed to figure out flights and spring break schedules. Be patient, Megan. One month later we hadn't sold a single ticket. Two months later, nothing. Three months later, not ONE FLIPPING TICKET SOLD.

How could this be? Where had we gone wrong? Was the world not ready for this? I had never launched an event with ZERO interest. For a hot minute, I felt like a failure. I was about to tell Alisa that we needed to cancel the whole plan. It obviously wasn't gaining any traction whatsoever. My brilliant idea started to seem no-so brilliant at all. *How was it that I got it so very wrong?*

I was torn. All the proof was telling me to cut my losses. A smart business person would see the signs, nix the plan and swallow the losses before causing any more financial and emotional hardship.

There was something big I was missing, but what was it? After some time, I returned to something I had told myself a long time ago, *When all else fails, go back to the mission. What do you stand for?* I took a deep breath and remembered my mission: women rising together. Instead of competition, we are our best when we lock arms.

I remembered my commitment, then. I remembered how it feels to be *aligned*, to be connected with other women who inspire. I remembered how it feels when you attend a retreat and hear the stories of other women. Even if just a weekend, I knew the journey that people would go through at Soul Success would be meaningful and maybe life-changing. I remembered the vision I had, bringing women from all walks of life together and connecting through story. It was going to be nothing short of *Magic*.

Next, I told my husband how frustrated I was that the event wasn't gaining traction. He's my best advisor because, unlike me, his answers are always so straight forward.

"Well, what are you doing at the event?" he asked.

"Hmmm.. I'm teaching yoga and speaking, and then Alisa is going to speak, too."

"Well, what's your point of the event?" Another great question.

"Women rising together."

"Rising together? Who's speaking? Do you have other speakers?"

Men are so simple. I fuckin' love the way their brain works.

"Duh!"

Women rising together... yes!

"Get speakers," he said. "It'll work."

At that point it was all about the Megan and Alisa show. We were the only speakers. People not buying tickets to the event was a little nudge from the universe that we were off course. We had to bring speakers and make this event a collaboration of women and the stories that made them who they are today.

So we got to work. I had no idea who these speakers were going to be, where they would come from, or what they would talk about. All I knew was that I needed them. So we posted online, open call for speakers, and what happened was nothing short of miraculous.

About a week later I logged online to see hundreds of women interested in speaking at the first Soul Success Summit. I may or may not have openly cried at my computer. These were women who believed in the mission. They believed in us. As I read through the applications, emotion overcame me. These women were exceptional. They were TEDx speakers, TV personalities, journalists, CEO's, philanthropists, and best-selling authors. I couldn't believe that they were asking if they could have the honor of speaking at *my* event. My mind was blown. I couldn't get my best friends or my own sisters to buy a ticket, but women from other continents with remarkable resumes were now applying to attend the event. I was stunned and inspired. That same feeling that I had when the idea crossed my mind was finally validated.

Our first event hosted women from all over the globe. They were best-selling authors, CEO's, fitness experts, therapists, entrepreneurs, philanthropists, PR experts, marketing experts, yoga teachers, jewelry designers. Their stories were moving. I got chills listening to how they started their businesses. They were all speaking the same language.

We were aligned, and our connections grew as we listened to each other's stories, as we each became a part of a new story.

After the event we stayed in touch through our Facebook group. I would see these women often in person, but it wasn't just me who stayed connected. It was the entire group traveling together, creating businesses together, interviewing one another on their podcasts, sharing their struggles, and supporting one another in countless ways. We all developed massive, legit crushes on each other. We were INSPIRED. Their successes were my success, and this feeling would continue to grow. We were rising together.

As I write this, I'm in the process of hosting the 5th Soul Success Summit. Since that first event, we've hosted women from all over the world as speakers, authors, vendors, leaders, and attendees. We've been a part of one another's lives and we've touched each other in ways I've never experienced before. Being a woman today is hard enough. Running a business is hard enough. Blend those two things together, and support is not just a recommendation. It's a requirement.

So at this point I'd like to step off my soapbox and have you meet the Soul Success sisters. Throughout the book we are going to share with you stories based on the Five Pillars of Soul Success. These pillars were created after listening to the stories and hearing these women speak to our audience. The Pillars can be looked at as five pieces to the life puzzle: Entrepreneurship and Leadership, Spirituality, Relationships, Health, and Money.

Similarly, this book is organized in five sections to embody the Five Pillars of Soul Success. As you begin to read, you'll find that each pillar is multi-dimensional and non-exclusive. In other words, they mutually benefit one another. In my experience, I have found it helpful to focus on one pillar at a time. I invite you to determine which of these pillars you want to focus on in your life right now.

Having it all perfect, all the time, isn't realistic. There are areas in our life that become our priority. One year your business and leadership skills might be the most important thing for you, but at the end of the year, perhaps you realize that in pursuit of your leadership success, your relationships have taken a backseat. So, next year, your focus turns to enhancing your relationships. While we may not have all Five Pillars perfected all the time, my wish is that you find balance and fulfillment through this work. My wish for you is that you no longer find yourself suffering in business, spirituality, relationships, money, or health because of the tools you gained right here.

CHAPTER 2

Women, Whooooa-Man!

I once met a woman at a business conference who described her business to me. She said, "I am a personal trainer for women. But don't worry, it's not like I'm a feminist or anything." I was baffled by this comment. Since when did empowering women become a bad thing? Feminism can seem like a dirty word that paints the picture of angry women who hate men.

I don't see it that way.

Webster's Dictionary defines feminism as the theory of the political, economic, and social equality of the sexes. This includes men as much as it includes women. I see feminism as an opportunity to celebrate women and men alike: to celebrate humans as loving equals. This is not just about women. It's about men too. The more that we enroll men in the conversation, the more powerful we as a human race all become-rising together. Misogyny is fueled by the misconception that feminists hate. I would like to be a part of the solution; a mission that clarifies what feminism really is and what it stands for: love and equality.

Men need us as equals. They need us in power, just as much as we need them. From the way I see it, the most powerful movements happen when it is fueled by the energy of love, acceptance, and inclusion. This is Soul Success.

It's pretty wild to think that everything I do is centered around women because to be completely honest, I used to feel threatened by many of them—in fact, my language may or may not have been stronger than that. It wasn't until my mid-twenties that I began to realize that the only one who suffers is the person hating and everyone else doesn't know or care. When people hate, it's often a reflection of how they feel about themselves, not what they claim they hate.

I wasn't this way with *all* women, though. My mom is a saint. You think I'm joking but she is, and her name is Theresa. She is the second coming of Mother Theresa. *Cue the choir music and release the doves.* In almost four decades, I've never heard my mother talk ill about anyone, or anyone talk ill about her. She has gone out of her way to be of service to others. From volunteering, to hosting parties, and baking cakes for people she hardly knew, attending every sporting and academic event that involved her four daughters, she was (and still is) always thinking of others. She makes people feel loved and celebrated. It doesn't matter who you are, how old you are, where you came from, or what you do. Everyone is important to my mother.

My sisters were also exceptions to my feelings about other women. When I say that I grew up with three sisters, people immediately begin to think of all the hair-pulling, along with the stolen tee shirts and boyfriends. My childhood was the exact opposite, probably due to the fact that my sisters and I are all spread apart, age-wise, so we never had mutual-friend drama. We're pretty mellow when it comes to drama in general. We have my parents to thank for that, because we were always told that there were more important things to focus on. My father is a sportswriter, so no surprise that we grew up playing sports and climbing trees.

I love my mother and sisters to the moon and back. I trust them with everything.

The ill feelings about girls and women began in 3rd grade with several negative encounters with my teacher, a woman. It continued in 6th grade with girls who made fun of me in the yearbook, and carried through middle school and high school where, for no good reason, my best friends would pretend I didn't exist. This cycle of distrust and competition repeated until my mid-twenties where a woman in corporate competing for the same job got me fired, and a fellow personal trainer placed a vendetta against me at a figure fitness competition. All of these experiences happened because we felt threatened by one another.

The vicious cycle of disloyalty and talking behind one another's backs continued throughout my life until I realized the one common factor in all of my horrible experiences with women was not them, it was me.

It was time for me to do some work on myself to stop this cycle. It was time for me to start loving and celebrating women, just like they deserve to be. Just like I deserve to be.

After I gave birth to my first daughter, I vividly remember holding her and thinking "You're gonna be fucked." I already felt sorry for her and her future girl-drama and petty high school bullshit. For a brief moment I wished she could be a boy so she wouldn't have to experience the heartache that I did. How sad for me to think those things. I didn't want that to be her reality. I didn't want her to feel bad about herself because her best friend one day, for no good reason, would decide that she just didn't like her anymore. I didn't want her to think that kind of behavior is okay—to dump friends just because your other friends don't approve. Boys don't do that (that was my impression, at least), so why do girls do it?

As a brand new mom, I was tired, emotional, and in physical pain; my nipples were still bleeding from nursing, and I hadn't pooped in a week. (Yep, those are the things they don't tell you before you have babies. You're welcome.) But Mykala was beautiful and innocent. She was pure. She hadn't committed any sins yet.

Not like her mother. Wink.

Then I started thinking about what a bitch I was in high school. I started thinking about all the competition. I had to be the best in everything and if I wasn't the best, I had to be better than most of my friends to be important. The sad reality is that while I was really good at a lot of things, I never really felt like I was the best at any one thing. I was a Division 1 athlete, I had boyfriends, I had good grades, but there was always a girl who was prettier, smarter, more athletic, and funnier than I was.

The culture of competition that tells young girls and boys that they have to be the best is still a living, breathing beast. The other day I got my daughter's standardized testing results, and even knowing what I just said to you, as a parent, I was so excited to share her results with my family. She is a little smarty pants and scored far higher than I ever did on tests. I was proud. But shouldn't I be proud of her anyway? Even if she scored low on every subject? Couldn't she still be brilliant? As a parent, of course, my answer is yes. But society doesn't look at it that way.

When I used to work as a school counselor in the LA Unified School District, I was trained to look at these scores and determine what was wrong with the child if they fell below average. But what if nothing was wrong with the child? What if algebra just wasn't their jam and they excelled in other things that a standardized test couldn't measure? What if they really wanted to play volleyball but they didn't make the team because there were twelve other girls who were better, taller, stronger, faster than her? Should she never have the chance to play volleyball?

We are doing a major disservice to our kids with the never-ending grading, testing, and competition. This culture perpetuates into adulthood. Prior to my business and leadership company, I built a successful network marketing business. We had an office and eventually opened nutrition and fitness centers across the West Coast. Toward the end of every month, the team gathered to see who was performing at the top of the organization. If you didn't make it to the Top 10, then you basically sucked that month. People would think and even *say* things like "What happened to you? What went wrong? Do you need help?" I was told this often by some of my mentors while showing me the numbers from the top performer that month. "If you want to make it to the next level, you have to do what Tom is doing. Look at his numbers! He is killing it!"

But what if I didn't want to do what Tom was doing? What if Tom was a dick? I don't want to be Tom.

We created promotions and if you didn't qualify for them, then something was off. And if you happened to be #1 that month, then you were a real life-breathing unicorn. Everybody wanted to be your friend, comb your hair, and smell your rainbow farts.

So if you wanted to be a unicorn, you had to be better than everybody else. I don't know anyone who doesn't want to be a unicorn so that was the goal for all of us. Were we supportive of one another? We had incredible tools and training programs that lifted everyone together. But still, even though we were a "team," the best was always the unicorn. You had to be better than everyone else, especially the person sitting next to you.

Now I'm not saying that the world should never have competitions. As an athlete and sports enthusiast, that would suck. Hard work and skill deserve to be celebrated. But I am suggesting that we've overdone it. Constantly pinning girls and boys against one another is giving us the false belief that if you want to make an impact, you have to be the best. And if you aren't, then you don't make the team.

A friend of mine told me the other day that during her parent-teacher conference, the teacher selected an exam from another student and said "Your daughter is low performing. We want her to be doing more work like this, and she's just not there yet." She was comparing her students. It's not the teacher's fault. Based on what I've heard, the teacher is amazing. As a past teacher and counselor, believe me, I appreciate and celebrate teachers. Their work is harder than many of us imagine. She's doing her job and her job at that time was to improve her students' test scores. She is trained to look at examples of how her students should perform. But can you imagine being told your child should be more like the others? Can you imagine what it would feel like if the low-performing student was in the room and heard this comment? She would have translated those words in her own way, possibly feeling like I did when a teacher once told me my ideas were stupid. She would have felt like she was not enough, she was inadequate, she was inferior. I know this student well and she is brilliant, soulful, and beautiful. Instead of comparing her to other kids and their performance in the classroom, we should be celebrating her gifts and offering support in the areas she needs.

We need more opportunities for inclusion, collaboration, and celebration. We need more ways for our youth to make the team, even if they aren't the best. We need more opportunities for adults to experience success even if they aren't the top producer in their organization. So you're not the best at volleyball, maybe others can lock arms with you and still invite you to play. Finding more ways for humans to collaborate and share their gifts will result in a positive impact. Our planet depends on it. We need more tools to rise together.

CHAPTER 3

The Women of Soul Success

As I began collecting these incredible memoirs from some of my closest female friends, I couldn't help but think about the apparent irony of it all. I went from harboring dislike and jealousy for women to now sharing their stories with the world.

These women have had to overcome barriers to become who they are today. As a sociologist and counselor, I realize that it actually isn't ironic at all. I am trained to look at people and study why they make the decisions they do and become who they are. I say this with all the love I have: My entire schooling was based on exploring why we're all so fucked up.

Women sometimes do some awful things to one another. We steal each other's boyfriends, we decide that for no good reason we just don't want to be friends anymore, we push each other down on the basketball court, we shame the woman on TV because we don't agree with her wardrobe choices or political agendas, and we compete against each other in every area of our lives—from our shoes, to our hair, to our parenting, to our careers—and it comes at a cost to all of us. Our culture tells us that we have to be at the top of our class, make it to the starting team, and race to the finish line in order to be somebody. We look at rank, grades, and statistics as the primary signs of accomplishment. If we want to be successful, we have to be better than everyone.

And I think it's necessary to mention that the more I study this, men do, too, in different ways. But that conversation's for another book, my friend.

Ladies, we have suffered enough. We still carry with us the trauma that our ancestors had to experience when we were powerless and voiceless. We still hold the grief that came from previous generations that required us to become subservient, second-class citizens. We used to be persecuted for having a voice, sometimes even to the point of death.

Times have changed. Now that we are beginning to be heard, we can't afford to step on one another. The world desperately needs more women in power and the only way we can accomplish that is by working together, not by letting our insecurities manifest in the countless forms of hating other women. I've witnessed countless women shaming other women in power. Shaming Lady Gaga for not having a six-pack, shaming JLO and Shakira for dancing too sexy, shaming the women who run for Presidential office, and shaming any woman who is brave enough to be visible.

This isn't about politics. This isn't about music or entertainment. It's about women supporting women. You don't have to vote for them if you don't agree with them, but don't blast them on social media because you're the very reason why only 25% of those who sit on Congress are women, 30% act as university presidents, 22% sit as Fortune

500 board members, and only 5% of these Fortune 500 CEO's are women (PEW Research Center).

We are half the population but we have less than 30% of the decision-making power. If we want this to change, we need to work together. We need to create a new standard for women. We need to *do better.*

Instead of criticizing the women who are visible, let's celebrate them for having the courage to stand up. We need to rewrite this story for future generations. When we see a woman on stage, let's compliment her instead of calling her a slut or a bitch. We don't have to always agree with what they have to say, but we do need to show them the same respect we want for our daughters. We must create this new standard because every time we shame a woman on a platform, we are telling young girls that this is what happens when you take a stand. I hope to God that when my daughters are on stage, they aren't called names for sharing their voice, but praised for their bravery. Praised for the courage it takes to stand up on a platform. Praised for whom they are.

There are women doing some beautiful things right now. The shakti, divine feminine power is rising. Just like anything, contrast brings opportunity for expansion, and I believe that we are at the beginning of a huge breakthrough for women in power. There are communities of women all over the world locking arms and lifting each other up. This is the mission behind Soul Success. We need to rewrite the narrative that says you need to compete against another woman to rise up. I have experienced, firsthand, that we can rise to greater heights when we have the courage to lock arms.

CHAPTER 4

The School Newspaper

"The pessimist complains about the wind.
The optimist expects it to change.
The leader adjusts the sails."
–John Maxwell

I f you would have asked me in high school to sign up for a leadership class or speak on stage, I would have said you got the wrong gal. Deep down, I wished I would have had what that role required. Some part of me wanted to be in front of a room informing, entertaining, and inspiring others. In high school, though, I didn't have the confidence or the courage or the self-esteem to put myself out there. But it wasn't always that way.

I was very loud when I was a little girl. I was constantly performing for other people as a way to share my gifts with the world. Everyone around me praised this part of me, which gave me permission to perform as much as possible. I can remember how important I felt during my grandmother's formal cocktail parties. She would invite all of her retired friends over to her house. At this point you could always find me wearing a pink or purple tutu. From the minute we showed up, I would beg my mother for the chance to perform. I counted down the minutes. My parents would make me wait until later in the evening, probably because they wanted to get everyone nice and liquored up to prepare them for what they were about to experience. Finally, once I got the green light, I would interrupt the social time and say these very words: *"Hey everybody! Stop your talkin' and start your watchin!"*

I lived for that moment.

I would make my mom press *play* and then it would begin: classical music would blare from the speakers as I would dance, sing, prance, twirl, tap, and tumble. I wasn't particularly talented, but it didn't matter. I felt like Madonna. In fact, I'm pretty sure I *was* Madonna, And the world *needed* to see me because I was amazing. I knew that my dancing was making people happy. I was entertaining people by expressing myself the best way I knew how. I felt important and celebrated.

When little kids share what lights them up, it doesn't matter whether or not they are talented. We love their ability to express and it makes us happy because it reminds us of something true inside of who we are, devoid of ego. We remember what it feels like to share our voice without judgment.

This is what was happening. I wasn't particularly talented. I had no rhythm, no strategy, no thought at all to my choreography. I was simply dancing to the beat of my own drum without a care in the world, and they loved it, because for a minute, it reminded them of their own inner child. It reminded them of a time in their life where they could do whatever they wanted and knew they would be loved and appreciated.

We have zero expectations for babies and toddlers. When they fall and bump their heads, we don't say "Watch where you're going! What's wrong with you? Can't you walk already?" And babies really don't care when they fall. They get right back up and try again. Imagine if babies stopped believing they could walk after their first fall, or that they could never pee in the potty because they ruined mommy's precious rug on the first try. We'd all be adults crawling around on the floor, shitting our pants. Kids are resilient and we teach them to be that way. But as we grow older, we start holding them and ourselves to a higher standard. We start to press our expectations onto other people.

I'm disappointed in you.

Ugh. I'm guilty of saying this to my seven-year old. It's a term many parents use, and it makes sense when our kids don't obey the rules. But if we use it over and over again, sometimes the child eventually begins to feel like they *are* a disappointment.

I can't remember my parents using that term very often when I was a little kid, so I believed I could be and do anything. They celebrated my quirkiness and always made me feel special.

Sometimes we give up on the first try because we fell.

My first experience that I can remember falling was in the 3rd grade. I had an incredible 2nd grade teacher who celebrated all of my ideas so, naturally, when I entered the 3rd grade I still believed I was a god. One day, I had an idea to start a school newspaper. I wanted to have a vehicle to share my voice and to give other kids the same opportunity. That newspaper was all I could think about. My father and his father wrote for a newspaper, so I would be the first woman in the family to continue the legacy. I imagined the look on my parents' faces when they opened this newspaper and saw my byline, just like daddy. I started writing those ever-important 3rd grade articles in my head. "Why handball is cool today," and "What was that mystery meat in the cafeteria?" You know, really important 3rd grade stuff.

I was so proud of myself and my idea. I couldn't wait to share it with my teacher. She would eat that shit up, and I would be her favorite student because I had the courage to start a newspaper. Giddily, I approached her to express my idea. And her response was something I've never forgotten. It still haunts me to this day. "You want to do what?" she said. "A newspaper? Sorry, honey but that's a stupid idea. Who has time for that? Absolutely not. We can't do that."

It was the first time in my life that I can remember feeling defeated. I went from feeling like a god—a natural born leader—to feeling like a piece of shit. I didn't know what that felt like until that very moment. It wasn't like I broke the seal of low self-esteem and hatred against women in a millisecond, but it was the beginning of a dark path for me.

The rest of that year was difficult. I felt my input and participation were not celebrated in any way. My teacher shot down my ideas all the time. When we were sharing our ideas for Show and Tell, I thought of my big sister, Amy, who was smart, driven, and nine years older than me, aka super-duper cool. I told my teacher I was going to bring my older sister's high school diploma to promote her as my mentor. She said, "People graduate from high school all the time. Bringing a diploma is silly. Find a better idea." Another situation that left me feeling disappointment and stupidity.

I let her get to me. I let her take my power away. I gradually stopped speaking in class. I stopped raising my hand, embarrassed of what people might say. This continued throughout elementary school. I would find confirmation for my stupidity, and instead of putting myself out there, I would hide in a corner to shield the risk of complete embarrassment. I lived my life to prove that my teacher was right: I was stupid. I let these feelings guide me for decades.

I let others steer my fate. I lost faith in myself because I let a few situations determine my worth. I don't think my teacher was trying to be malicious. I don't think she actually thought I was stupid. I later learned that her responses to my ideas had nothing to do with me. She experienced significant trauma that year as her husband had just passed away. And if we know anything about trauma, we know that people process it in different ways. I'm certain that she was not trying to make me feel bad. I'm certain that she did not understand the power behind her words and how it would influence me for coming years.

And that's exactly why it's important for us to share our stories and tools with one another. Everyone experiences trauma at some point. And I'm not just referring to the trauma my teacher experienced losing her husband. I'm also referring to the psychological trauma I experienced when I interpreted those words she employed. Sometimes we think that trauma needs to be a result from a catastrophic event, but the word literally means "wound." Trauma is not defined by the actual event but from the psychological impacts it brings. It comes in different forms and levels. It might be a feeling of abandonment because your mother worked long hours and you thought she might never come back. It might come in the form of physical trauma from a near-death experience you can't avoid reliving. Or, as with me, it might be a misinterpretation of something someone said, and you live your life to prove they were right.

Becoming a leader doesn't mean you have to own a Fortune 500. It means living a life of positive influence. You could be a public speaker or a best-selling author, or you could be someone who leads others in your community by silent action; people want to become better just by being in your presence. You might already be living each day as a leader in your community.

If you want to be a leader but don't feel like you can, my hope is that you unlock the wound in your life that's misinforming you.

It's time, my love.

It's time for you to rewrite the story that you can't or shouldn't be. I said it before, and I'll say it again: I need you to know that you are more than enough. You deserve to take your power back.

Four Activities for Soul Success Leadership

1. Write down a moment in which you gave your power away to someone else. What happened?
2. What lesson did you learn from this experience?
3. What do you stand for?
4. Who can you ask for support when it comes to your vision?

PILLAR 1

Spirituality

*"Our whole spiritual transformation
brings us to the point where we realize that
in our own being: we are enough."*
- Ram Dass

Many people think that spirituality and success is all about love and light, or at least that's what I used to think. Yes, rainbows, unicorns, and butterflies are a huge part of being Soulfully Successful. I love unicorns and I hope to be one with my daughters someday. At the same time, confronting and working through our demons is the other huge side to transformation. I used to look at spirituality through the lens of "high vibes only." If it wasn't high-vibe, I wasn't touching it. All along, though, darkness was around me staring me straight in the face without me knowing. This is when I discovered the power behind shadow work. Confronting and working through our demons is the real magic of transformation.

I've gotten into a lot of shit in my life, but until I became aware of its source, it just kept coming back in different forms.

Now I look at spirituality as alignment not just with yourself, but with the universe as a whole. The more spiritual work I do, the more awareness and light I harness. Spirituality tells us that we are all as one. We are all connected.

In this section, you'll hear stories from women who were able to channel that same power from the universe despite the odds against them. We are excited to leave you with tools to channel your own inner superpowers, the same that create worlds.

CHAPTER 5

Alchemy

J amie and I met at a business-and-money talk I was giving at the Ketchum Innovation Center. When I finished my talk, she approached me and said, "We need to work together." In a matter of minutes, I knew two things about Jamie. The first was that she is intuitive. People that are intuitive make decisions based on the heart. They don't overthink but act on what feels right. They trust their decisions because they trust their hearts and they don't look back. Looking back only leads to heartache and regret.

The second thing I knew about Jamie is that she had powerful gifts that needed to impact others on a massive scale. I wasn't yet clear on her story, but I knew that something profound was also calling me toward her. Her story is big but, for whatever reason, it was a secret. I had a strong and clear message that her gifts needed to be revealed. The secrets were *ready* to be revealed.

On a personal note, I also knew we would be fast friends. I could sense she was deeply connected and spiritual, but she also had a fun and quirky side.

When we hopped onto our first coaching call, she told me her story. It wasn't long before I got full body chills. What I love the most, though, is Jamie's ability to shift trauma consciousness to heightened spiritual consciousness. She is like an alchemist, and despite the heft of her story, it will leave you feeling light and powerful. Her connection to the divine, curiosity and connection with the non-physical will give you an enlightened perspective and tools to live by. I have no doubt you will fall in love with her, too.

Jamie Green

In a world where the current dominant systems and foundational pillars of societal structure program everyone into the normative acceptance of war, prejudice, discrimination, and intolerance, it's easy to see the massive piles of steaming shit that are everywhere. A world in which we are hardwired to suffer not only the collective trauma embedded into our subconscious minds, but the generational trauma, as well—the collective wounds that live in the very fabric of our DNA—the trauma is passed down from generation to generation for us to recreate in our own time and place in the culture-scape. There's individual trauma and interpersonal trauma which can have a generational aspect, as well. With all this human suffering it's almost hard to even imagine a world that isn't chock-full of these steaming piles of shit for everyone to smell, step in, track into the house. They can make us feel like our entire adult life is spent just trying to clean up all the shit and get rid of that God-awful smell.

I'm here to tell you that those piles of shit really do transform into nuggets of gold when we acknowledge them, face them, and then hold our noses and realize that they contain messages for us. I'm going to share with you some of the biggest flaming shit bombs that I've been hit with in this lifetime and I'll forewarn you that this one has been a doozy, but I'm here for it. I show up every day, fierce in my commitment to live from my heart and love all damn day.

My story begins with my birth. I was born three days after the tragic death of my two-year-old brother. He was walking down the sidewalk of our cul-de-sac when a neighbor backed her car out of her driveway and killed him. He was cremated on my birthday. I felt my mother's terror from her womb. I entered into a world full of trauma and grief. My parents and older brother and sister were literally trying to survive the utter devastation of this living nightmare. As little humans we have a lot of big emotions and needs. At times when I expressed those big feelings and asked for those needs to be met, or asked for playfulness and warmth and joy from my family, they often could not be present for me in that way. At times, and understandably so, it was simply too much to ask because of the devastating heartbreak they were living with. Their attention was focused on their own emotional coping and healing. It was all they could do to just get through the days that just keep coming, insensitive and unyielding to our wounds.

So begins what I have come to know as my life's defining story: when I'm a fully expressed person, with big uncomfortable feelings or needs, they are too much to handle, and the people I love and need the most will either pull away or dismiss my feelings. I came to learn that this pulling away felt like loss, like the death of my brother, and that losing people is terrifyingly painful. This is the core, defining story I made up in response to these painful life experiences. I also created coping mechanisms to protect my heart, to stay safe, to receive attention and feel loved. My strategy was to push my needs and big uncomfortable feelings to the side and be joyful, fun, and bring as much happiness as possible. Pretty ingenious really, these incredible nervous systems of ours.

When we are small children, we are building our foundation in the subconscious mind, learning about our environment based on feedback from our families and other prominent people, places, and experiences. We are wiring our brains and making decisions, creating stories that feel like truths, developing coping mechanisms to deal with painful emotions, and curating strategies that get us the attention and love we crave. It's what we do.

We bring this subconscious foundation we built with us and often spend most of our adult lives unlearning and releasing all those stories, coping mechanisms, and strategies that kept us feeling safe as children. We have no reason to blame, shame, or fault ourselves or others for the experiences any of us go through on our journey in this life. These are the families and experiences we came into this physical form to learn from, and with, in order to experience this incredible life.

Our life force, spirit, essence, soul, or whichever legend that describes your inimitable, energetic, quantum blueprint, comes into this physical form for the purpose of healing. We come with our own karma and dharma and soul contracts, and from the moment we are born we are walking our individual path of healing. We're all just doing our very best from our own level of consciousness, my family included. My mother, father, older brother and sister and younger brother, are the most amazing, loving, and brave people I know. Because we lived this trauma together, we were all affected by it in our own unique way, and we are surviving it together. Through this experience we touched Divinity. We know how to dig deep, we know how to love, and we don't take that love for granted. Hint hint…Gold.

As I grew, I had a profound sense of wonder about the meaning of life. One of my earliest memories is lying on my parents' bed while my mother sat next to me folding laundry. and asking her, "Why are we here?"

She finished folding a towel and said, "You're awfully young to ask such a big question." Then she said, "I don't know, Jamie. I guess that's what we're all here to figure out."

I also had keen intuition, a heightened awareness of people's energy and emotions, and I sensed energy moving, especially in the dark. I had dreams of things that were going to happen and then they would happen. At times, I knew what people were going to say before they said it. These qualities didn't really get much attention from me in childhood because I was just out in the world being a kid, playing, discovering, and exploring. But they ended up playing a key role in my life.

I have come to understand that we attract opportunities into our lives to address what needs healing. The stories that are streaming through us subconsciously will actually put our conscious mind to work to find confirmation for these stories in our daily experiences. So, with regard to the brain, our conscious mind is like a search engine exploring all the places where it can find more confirmation of these unconscious stories. These un-ending searches create energetic frequencies that attract the people and experiences we need to bring these subconscious stories into our conscious awareness to be recognized, released and healed. This is one facet of the law of attraction. So, throughout my life, I had more experiences that reaffirmed these unconscious stories of mine. My first boyfriend, who was also my best friend, died in a car accident when I was fourteen. The trauma, devastation, shock, grief, and loss were confirmed again.

At 19 years old, I decided to follow my keen intuition and enrolled in my first energy healing and massage classes. This led to coaching certification courses and classes on Divine feminine power and presence, energy healing, quantum physics, the law of attraction, and more. I took a quantum energy healing certification course which included a process that introduced us to one of our feminine spirit guides, and through this deeply personal and transformational process I was introduced to new realms that my mind could never have fathomed. For reasons I'll explain later, I'll tell you here that I discovered my guide in that course, a dolphin named Adina. I continued my pursuit of knowledge in the fields of metaphysics and the healing arts which evolved over the next five years into a Natural Health Practitioner degree and Usui Reiki Master Teacher attunement and certification. I was beginning to understand the power of our Divine energy, our source connection and the importance of all four bodies: physical, mental, emotional and spiritual. I began taking clients and as I was taking responsibility for my own life, walking the path of healing my own grief and trauma, I was also helping others to heal. Wink wink…more gold.

Fast forward to age thirty. I'm married to a musician and we have two beautiful children. The house we were living in at the time had a six-thousand square-foot yard. It was a beautiful layout and well maintained with a half basketball court, big trees, a vegetable garden, stone firepit, gazebo, jacuzzi and a koi pond surrounded by lush mature foliage. We spent a lot of time in that beautiful backyard.

One day I was out there doing yard chores and cleaning up while the kids were napping. I was trying to get as much done as I could in those precious few moments while both toddlers were sleeping and was moving quickly until, all of a sudden, I found myself standing trance-like in front of the koi pond. When I came out of my reverie, I wondered how long I had been there and what the heck urged me to just stand there, I had so much to do. On I went with the busy life of a mom with two toddlers and I didn't give too much thought to the occasion. But the same thing happened two more times over the next week. I was just being guided to the koi pond subconsciously, each time with the same mystified response from me.

Then came the day when the most defining event of my adult life occurred. It was a cool and cloudy winter morning in Southern California. My husband and I took our son, three, and our daughter, fourteen months, on a bike ride to the park. We had a lovely morning playing as a family. As we arrived home, in the reintegration of putting the bikes away and heading into the kitchen for lunch, the phone rang. It was my mother. While we were speaking, I looked around for my daughter. When I realized that neither my husband nor I had her with us in the kitchen, phone still in hand, I ran directly to the koi pond. I didn't even think to go anywhere else. I was guided there, as I had been guided three times that week. Within three minutes and thirty seconds, while transitioning from the bike ride to the kitchen, our daughter had slipped away to the koi pond in the back yard and fallen in. I found her face down, floating on top of the water. I screamed, throwing the phone down and smashing it to pieces. I jumped into the water in sheer panic to save my daughter. My mind went blank, and a feminine voice, crystal clear, spoke to me. "This is not the end," she said.

I reached my daughter and turned her over. Her face was blue. Foam dribbled from her mouth. My husband, who had run outside at the sound of my scream, took her from me. He started CPR while I scrambled to find another phone. As I completed the 911 call, I heard a blood-curdling scream from my husband and ran back out to them. Though he had cleared out all the water, she was not breathing. We took turns giving her CPR breaths and heart pumps until a police officer responded, leaping into action. We later learned that the officer had a daughter just a few months younger than ours. When he saw us at the pond, he saw his own family standing in front of him, and he would stop at nothing to help us save our child.

The paramedics arrived shortly thereafter and, as they were rushing my daughter out to the ambulance, my mother arrived and nearly fainted as she saw her on the gurney. I caught her and steadied her. Here the two of us were again, experiencing this terror together once more. Life the next few days were a blur. Time stopped, became completely irrelevant, a mere illusion until we learned that she would make a full recovery.

She had regained a faint heartbeat on the way to the hospital where the staff induced a coma. On her third day in the hospital, the results from her brain scans told us that she would make a full recovery and that, later that day, they would be able to bring her out of the coma they induced for many important reasons.

My husband left the hospital for the first time to go home for a shower and to bring me clean clothes. When he returned, he had an incredulous look on his face that I didn't understand. He pulled a piece of paper out of his pocket and told me that he found it on his desk. Scribbled on the paper were lyrics he had written the day before our daughter's accident. The lyrics read, "Lay my head upon the stone, Feel the water trickle through my bones, Through her whisper I awoke." Those lyrics later became a whole song called "Adina."

Seven days later we left the hospital with our beautiful daughter to finish her healing process in the comfort of our own home.

She's absolutely perfect and it's a complete miracle. There is no logical, medical reason that she is alive. The first officer didn't show up until nearly five minutes after we called. The paramedics took two more minutes to arrive and at least two more to get her into the ambulance. Along with whatever time she had spent in the pond, she had spent perhaps eleven minutes without breath or heartbeat.

From my perspective, the explanation is that she chose to live, and this life held this karma and dharma for us all to walk together, and we had plenty of help from the other side.

This experience took us from the seventh circle of hell to a deeply spiritual and miraculous paradise. Our daughter was alive.

It was also a major traumatic event, triggering PTSD and a period of nervous system hijacking. It was in fact the greatest invitation into healing my life. This is where radical self-responsibility becomes the only option and, as I have come to learn, is one of the keys to our salvation.

Over the last nine years I have faced this trauma head on, seeking out the knowledge, literature, courses, coaching, and therapy that have given me a comprehensive and esoteric understanding of the nervous system, attachment theory, somatic integration, embodiment, consciousness, and spiritual development and ascension.

The more responsibility I took for my healing, the more I unearthed from my subconscious programming, and the more I came to understand myself. The more I understood, the easier it was to hear these unconscious programs and limiting beliefs and bring them into conscious awareness. Opportunities arose to love myself, to stand in acceptance of exactly where I was in each moment and cultivate a new relationship with my consciousness.

Even though these moments haven't always been pretty, what I uncovered as I faced myself over and over again is that I got braver each time and realized that my painful experiences and traumas are actually my superpowers. I recognized that the coping mechanisms I created as a little girl were brilliant at keeping me feeling safe back then, and they served me very well. Those strategies helped shape me into a wonderful person with qualities that are some of my favorite attributes. Then came the realizations that those strategies had stopped keeping me safe and were actually holding me back and keeping me stuck in my old unconscious stories and pain body.

Here is where the perspective shifts. Here is where alchemy transforms pain into wisdom, piles of shit into nuggets of gold. These pains became my superpowers and they forced me into vulnerability. Being vulnerable with myself invited me to take ownership of my multi-dimensional self. I went into the depths of my shadow self, facing shame and rage and envy and neediness and all the unloved places within me. I met my inner child with love and compassion, seeing all the places she was acting out, hiding or rebelling, all out of longing for being heard, seen, loved, and accepted. I cultivated a relationship with my inner Divine Masculine and Feminine aspects. Here we hold so much collective and generational trauma.

Processing this wounding was deep and chaotic, and the healing attention was intensely imperative. Showing up to witness and heal these dimensions of myself, and giving myself the gift of time, presence, and attention, is what allowed me to connect with my higher self, which is the true source of our power. Here lies our Divinity, the essence to be devoted to. This is a place where we shine like a thousand stars, where our purpose connects directly to our heart, and we live and create our own heaven on Earth directly from the Divine source of unconditional love.

This is the place where bravery exists; this is the place where we allow ourselves to be fully expressed. It starts with us and then transmutes into service for all of humanity. This is where we get to share all of that gold with everyone else. It is an overwhelmingly life-changing thing when we can see ourselves as the Divine beings we are and can love ourselves enough to be vulnerable. We are not only in a deep state of self-care when we share our vulnerability, we are also in Divine service to inspire others to heal, to love themselves more deeply and feel seen and understood through our collective wounds and the common pain that unites us all. The amazing Brene Brown said, "Only when we are brave enough to explore the darkness will we discover the infinite power of our light."

This is MY power. My gift is in the sharing, just me, exactly as I am, facing myself, accepting myself, taking radical responsibility for myself, loving myself, and showing up—imperfections and all. As I show up just like this, the safer I feel, the more connected to my power I am, the more healing I gift myself. This allows me to extend the invitation to others to join me. To first show up for themselves and then allow themselves to witness their own healing and to perform the alchemy that transforms their pain into wisdom and wisdom into service. That's how we all turn piles of shit into nuggets of gold. This is how WE unite and rise together. This is how we heal collective trauma. This is how we transcend the current systems that perpetuate the wounds that divide us. This is how we harness our quantum aspects and ascend into higher frequencies and dimensions. This is where we have a massive impact and create the world in which WE want to live. This is also YOUR power.

We all have a purpose, we all have a voice, we are all here to be fully expressed and have an impact while living from our hearts and expressing our eclectic gifts and manifesting our creative desires in this life. We are all worthy, sovereign, Divine beings with gifts to explore and offer in service to ourselves, the Earth, and humanity. It's also meant to be fun as hell and full of love. Oh, and don't forget the orgasms… we're here for those, too.

As we take steps along our continued healing journey and are called more and more into the next highest version of ourselves, here are some of the techniques I utilize consistently. I hope they help to support you in your growth and ascension process. All that ascension means is simply raising your vibration to the next level of consciousness.

1. Take radical responsibility for your life. Your thoughts, emotions, and beliefs are already creating your life. The sooner you understand this and then show up for yourself fiercely, the sooner you step into unlocking your power.

2. Self-love all the fucking time. I mean every second of every day SELF-LOVE. When you're disappointed in yourself, self-love. When you screw the same thing up again, self-love. When you criticize and judge yourself, self-love. Actually say out loud, "I love myself, even when I'm judging and criticizing myself."

3. Acknowledge that where you are right now is exactly where you are meant to be and that these piles of shit are here to be transformed. Get your journal and write down one of the problems you would like to change, or a potential you would like to create. Get vulnerable with yourself here and allow yourself to witness and purge the underlying thoughts and emotions that have been the driving force behind the undesired limiting beliefs that have been holding you back.

4. Accept that you have been committed to the subconscious stories, coping mechanisms and limiting beliefs that have created this problem or have kept you from achieving a desired potential. Commit to changing those NOW! Speak your commitment out loud until you feel that you are committing in your heart, with your whole being.

5. Choose one way in which you are going to show up differently to begin to shift. Write down and say out loud the new mindset/perspective shift you are now

creating. Take this one action consistently! When you forget or catch yourself repeating the same old behavior, love yourself and say, "Thank you and cancel clear. Universe, God(dess) Spirit, (the Divinity that resonates with you), I release this old strategy to the universe." Then re-commit to the new action and belief system again and again and again.

CHAPTER 6

Owning Your Throne

I jokingly call Pirie my "Spirit Mom." But it's not so far from the truth. We met many years ago at a Christmas party shortly after I moved to Sun Valley. My mother-in-law kept telling me that we needed to connect because of our involvement in the wellness industry. Nobody in town knew who I was at that time and everybody knew Pirie Grossman.

Pirie was a TV personality, E! TV anchor, worked with the Dalai Lama, and Maya Angelou among many others, and curated the Sun Valley Wellness Festival. She was also one of the original G.L.O.W. Girls (Gorgeous Ladies of Wrestling). I started binge-watching the show on Netflix about the same time Pirie hired me to work with her. I became obsessed with the show and in my dreams would create a scenario in which I was a famous female wrestler in the 80's. I had no clue I was actually coaching one! So when you're reading her story, you can imagine this lovely lady doing body slams in an American flag leotard. It's quite possibly the best thing ever.

One time at dinner, she casually mentioned that Johnny Cash was her Godfather. Johnny fucking Cash. Okay, how ironic is this? As I type this, I just right now realized that

I'm wearing a Johnny Cash tee shirt. Yeah, for real. Signs everywhere? If Pirie is my Spirit Mom and Johnny Cash is her Godfather, does that make him my Great Spirit Godfather? One could only hope. Pirie is a living breathing wellness rockstar. So naturally, I've always had her on my radar.

A few years after we met, she asked me to coffee to see if I could help her launch her new coaching business. You could imagine my excitement getting the chance to work with a wellness rockstar. I mean, how many people do you know have had the chance to work directly with the Dalai Lama, Maya Angelou, and can call Johnny Cash their Godfather? I was confident that her next stage in business was going to be exceptional.

What I didn't realize is how much Pirie, in turn, would work magic on me. She has come to be a trusted advisor, confidante, and spiritual mentor. She has helped me navigate through different energies, giving me tools to protect myself, to access my inner light. She has a heart of Gold. I've witnessed her light magic as she has helped others heal the trauma in their lives. I'm so excited for you to meet her, too.

Pirie Grossman

My story begins on a hazy, late August afternoon when I returned home from my fertility doctor's office in Pasadena, California after he had extracted eggs from my uterus for the seventh time in eight months. This extraction is part of the process known as in-vitro fertilization or IVF. The lab mixes my husband's semen with my eggs with the hope of creating healthy embryos to be transferred to our surrogate. Blindsided by my inability to carry a pregnancy, my husband and I remained hopeful that our surrogate—a healthy

26-year-old who had previous success carrying two babies for another couple—could carry our baby. This was the second time we transferred our embryos into this surrogate. She was our second surrogate.

I was 37, my husband was 42. We had been together for four years when we decided to get married. We were in love and giddy with the thought of having a child. Steve had a fabulous daughter, and I loved them both with all my heart. They were the reason I wanted to become a mother. Their beautiful relationship inspired me to have a child. We were excited about growing our family.

At the doctor's office, after my seventh extraction was complete, we returned home where I climbed into bed to rest. My husband went to work, and our housekeeper took care of me. My body, mind, and spirit were exhausted. I felt depleted, yet optimistic. Maybe this time our surrogate would get pregnant. I soon fell asleep, dreaming of a healthy pregnancy.

Within a few hours, I woke up with severe nausea and cramps. I felt weak and dizzy, and when I stood to walk to the bathroom, my world went dark. I'm not sure how long I was on the floor or who even found me. All I remember is waking up in an emergency room, my body burdened by tubes and a headache so mind-numbing it felt as though a hatchet had been left in my head. My husband was standing beside my bed, holding my hand with a look on his face that struggled to adequately describe my situation. My sister was also in the room, whispering into the phone. I later learned that she and my husband were conferring as to what to do. I felt lifeless. All I wanted to do was sleep. The next time I awoke, I was in a different hospital. I had been transported across town from the Huntington in Pasadena to Cedars Sinai in Los Angeles.

My internist informed me I had lost a massive amount of blood and within the last 48 hours had received three blood transfusions. I continued to hemorrhage. I was now in the ICU and soon would be prepped for surgery to correct the tear in my uterine wall.

I was so thoroughly exhausted I slept for another three days. When I finally woke, my weight had plummeted to 100 pounds. I saw Steve's face leaning over me, his eyes squinting in distress. He told me that he was worried he was losing me. He wanted me to give up trying to have a baby. I didn't think I could feel worse, physically or mentally, yet my chest tightened with every word, pushing my heart up to the back of my throat where it burned like an uncontrolled forest fire. I felt like a failure.

Forty-eight hours later, my husband brought me home. My body—achy and riddled with vast amounts of fertility drugs, as well as sleeping, pain, and anti-anxiety medications—was a numbed reminder of the hospitals in which I had taken residence for twelve days. The lingering depression had wrapped itself tightly around me, forbidding me to react to anything other than where I might next curl up in a fetal position and drift away.

What came next, I could have not predicted. As I lay in bed, trying to heal in my own way from this short-circuited and dangerous attempt at motherhood, my husband announced that he needed a break. He and his daughter were headed to our home in Sun Valley, Idaho. He asked me if I wanted to join. It seemed like a bad joke. How could I? I could barely walk. My doctor gave me stern instructions that included round-the-clock bed rest. Travel was out of the question.

In the brief time he spent thinking about the events that had interrupted our IVF cycle, Steve became cold and indifferent. Something had changed the man I loved; this man was a stranger to me. He insisted I stop trying to have a baby and that he and his daughter needed to be enough for me. He missed his life—our life. In a clipped tone, typically reserved for his business affairs, he said he didn't like who I had become. The words burrowed into my vacant body. Nothing was making sense. There was a distance between us that I'd never encountered with him. He had always taken care of me. He was that kind of husband. But this man had shut down and was unsympathetic to my pain, my health, my well-being. I didn't feel an ounce of compassion or love from him. I remember thinking that we might not make it—a thought that had once been inconceivable. How could I live without him? He and his daughter were my family. And then the real pain inside me, in my heart, became insufferable.

He turned away, walked out of our bedroom, and left. His casualness only exacerbated my confused and lonely reality. There was no one in our home to help me. Within moments of his departure and absence, I felt a noticeable shift in my state of mind. Despair had become my new partner; I knew I was in trouble.

My sister called to check on me. I told her what had happened and she rushed over, furious to hear that my husband left me alone. She said she would stay with me until he returned.

Over the course of a couple of days, I learned more about my experience at Cedars-Sinai. My sister said that my doctor told her they almost lost me twice.

"Your sister is very strong on the inside," he had said, "But her body is weak."

He agreed I should take a break from trying to have a baby.

During that Labor Day weekend, I was alone in my thoughts. Not once did my husband call or check on me, and I felt the sting of his negligence from afar. He was pulling away from me physically, emotionally, and mentally. With that, I detached from the rhythms of normalcy. I subconsciously staged my own disappearing act; slipped into a dark and disconnected place, away from everyone I knew and loved. All I could think about was how I was such a failure. I couldn't create a baby. Not only could I not get pregnant, but neither could our surrogates, who each tried twice. At that time, I had never considered my husband's virility. My fertility specialist paraphrased numerous times that I was too old and so were my eggs. I was judging myself so harshly for not being able to create life, and now I was the one responsible for my marriage being in shambles. My hopes and dreams vanished, they were replaced with helplessness and hopelessness.

Family and friends knew me as strong. I could get up time and time again through any failure. I'd try again with a big smile on my face. I was the perky girl! Nothing could keep me down. I had faith in God and believed that bad would change to good with His divine power and I preached that belief to everyone. I always carried hope in my heart, no matter what. But this grief was unlike anything I had experienced. I plunged into an even darker place, desperately looking for the light inside of me. Where was God? I prayed for the excruciating pain to be taken away from me. The drugs removed any sense of self I had. I didn't know who I was or what I was doing anymore. As I was spiraling emotionally at a rapid rate. My husband returned home. It was the night of Labor Day, September 7, 1998.

I was sleeping on our leather sofa in our media room, the TV my constant companion when I heard the back door of our garage open. As he walked in and sat down on the sofa, he asked how I was feeling. Surprisingly, I was happy to see him. Maybe he would be kinder? I could scarcely lift my head off the sofa, and when I reached out for a hug or a kiss, he backed away. We had always been habitually affectionate toward each other, but now those affirming touches and nods ceased to exist. He stood and walked as far away from me as the room would allow.

I tried to catch my breath before he asked me if I had given any thought to his request that we stop trying to have a child. I said yes, I did. I said I would be willing to if we could consider adoption. He glared at me with disdain and laughed. He said he would never consider that as an option. And how could I want someone else's child?

He told me that while he was in Sun Valley he had time to think about what he wanted, and confessed he didn't want a child anymore. He claimed the sole reason he married me was because we were going to have a child together, and he wanted to make sure the child had his name. But since that wasn't going to happen for us, he wanted a divorce.

I felt my body tremble with the rush of adrenaline and then I didn't hear anything else he said. He was throwing our marriage and me away. Nothing seemed real. My head whirled with confusion and my heart pinched with anticipation. A light-headedness nipped at my vision as the pressure of all the drugs in my body began heating up and coursing furiously in my veins. This couldn't be happening! I couldn't take any more grief and sadness. I felt as though I didn't exist any longer and that unsteady sensation was the light leaving me.

I was standing in front of a man I didn't know. Where was my husband? This man was dismissive, deliberate, and deadly—his tapestry of venomous words and actions prompted my eruption. I told him I didn't want a child anymore! I only wanted him and our marriage. I'd promise to give up my dream and start being the woman he wanted again. "Please take me back," I pleaded. He stood like a tower in front of me, his voice calculating, his body rigid.

"No," he said. He had made up his mind. He wanted a divorce and that was it. I begged him to give us another chance. How could his feelings for me vanish over two days? We shared a passionate marriage for four years. How could he discard me so quickly?

"Give me a chance to heal," I said. "And let's go to therapy. We could work this out." He stood motionless; his head and neck stiff, his eyes locked on the wall behind me. I walked over to him and said, "I thought you loved me?"

"I don't love you anymore," he said. "Not *this* Pirie, the woman who's sick and weak. I miss the fun, sexy woman who was full of life."

I missed her, too.

"You should go to Houston and be with your parents," he said. "I'll talk with my attorney tomorrow morning and start the divorce proceedings. Good night."

Whatever was left holding me up at that moment came crashing down. I started shaking, fell back on the sofa, and became sick. The tears flowed. Everything had been taken away from me. My life had disintegrated. I felt like garbage being tossed out of my own home. So this is what it felt like to be nothing to someone you thought would love you forever. I was nothing and this nothing was being told to leave tomorrow. I could hardly even stand up.

Then a thought occurred. I looked at the seven bottles of medications sitting on the table in front of me. I would go to sleep. It would be painless. And then I wouldn't have to feel this agonizing pain any longer. I opened the bottles and swallowed over 250 pills. I lay down, then, and told God I was coming home and closed my eyes.

"Now I lay me down to sleep, I pray the Lord my soul to keep, and if I die before I wake, I pray the Lord my soul to take."

A violent bout of vomiting woke me. Somehow, I was in our bed, and my husband was holding me trying to stop the convulsions. There were people in the room yelling out to each other. I was being picked up and moved to another bed. Then it went dark.

Days later, I learned I had returned to Cedars Sinai hospital, my home away from home. It was a repeat performance; my husband standing next to my bed, staring at me with that same worry. His voice rose as he called for a nurse. He told me I was lucky to be alive.

My thoughts came rushing in, why was I in the hospital again? I didn't remember that I tried to take my life until a mental health provider arrived. She was gentle and asked many questions. Then I remembered, and shame and guilt scorched my heart and soul. Hot tears streaming down my face and quickly turned into the sobs of a wounded animal. The shame was unbearable. How could I have done that? My husband was right. I needed to give up my dream of being a mother. I couldn't even take care of myself. It wasn't meant to be.

For the first few days of my hospital stay, Steve visited every day. Relentless, he continued asking me if I was going to stop trying to have a baby. I said yes, but on the third day I brought up adoption again. He recoiled, and with his eyes blazing, said, "Absolutely not!" The subject changed to divorce, but he said we would talk about it when I got better. With that, he turned around and walked out of my hospital room for the last time.

Two days later I called my sister who brought me home. When I arrived, I went back to bed so I could lay down. I called my parents and made arrangements to fly to Houston the next day. Steve was home but sleeping in another bedroom.

The next morning as I packed, Steve entered our bedroom. He said his attorney had prepared divorce papers. He hoped it wouldn't get messy and offered a mediator if I wanted one to assist in the negotiations. He uttered that he would be fair. I was stunned by his ruthlessness.

Yet some light inside of me had switched on. Even through the pain, I felt peace. I had survived. God was with me and had a plan and purpose for my life.

I flew to Houston the following day and stayed with my parents for two weeks. I spent time with my sister, my brother and his family. They prayed with me every day. They didn't give up on me as my husband had, and even as I had.

The first part of my healing was realizing that I had given my worthiness away—I had to find self-love. I reconnected to my spiritual side, my faith. I found great strength from God every day. I grew stronger and started to heal physically and mentally. God spared my life and I felt an overflow of gratitude. I had been given a second chance, and now I needed to find out why. I would embark on a new life journey.

Where would I go next?

A vision came to me. Move to Sun Valley, Idaho.

And so I did.

The energy of the mountains became my refuge. That energy reaffirmed who I was, where I had been, and who I could become. It restored my worth.

Within a year, I met a beautiful man who loved me and wanted to fulfill my dream of being a mother. We created two healthy children. My dream had come true! Now, my 16-year-old son and 14-year-old daughter are the heartbeats of my life. I even beat the odds by having them when I was 44 and 46 years old!

Let's connect and conclude the story as far as my ex-husband is concerned. Steve passed away from liver cancer nine years after we divorced. If we had had children together, I would be a widow and our children wouldn't have a father. We made our peace and forgave one another before he passed. Our karma is done. My children met him and he was genuinely happy for me.

What is the moral of the story for me?

Never. Give. Up.

Not on dreams, or goals, or plans, or marriage, or happiness, or children. Trust yourself, even when it becomes challenging, complicated, and grim. And never give away your precious life. Situations change. People change. Give yourself time. Reach out for help and let others know when you are in a dark place. I didn't. I kept the pain inside me.

I was ashamed that I wasn't strong enough. The light we need when we can't find it within is outside—in our relationships, our family, our friends. Their light will turn your light on because of the love and connection with other souls. We need each other to survive.

You are not alone. Do not hide. Do not isolate yourself.

Trust your inner compass. It's your soul giving you directions. That still and small voice that's loving and compassionate is your guide. Don't allow others to discount or negate your dreams. They may have their own, which is fine, but your dreams are *yours*. They deserve an opportunity to grow, to be realized, and to be shared.

God believed in me, as I know he does you. This part of my life was the most demanding lesson thus far. I learned I could count on myself to reach a place where my gratitude for life *changed* my life. I was spared and I'm here to share my story with you.

Now you know the real reason I've been an advocate for people to not take their lives; and why I started a task force in my community to lower the high suicide rates in our state. I am that survivor. I am that woman who doubted her worth. I am that woman who forgave herself and renewed her self-love.

For a long time, I had kept this part of my life a secret because I was embarrassed. But I'm not anymore. What I considered to be my weakness is actually my greatest strength. I love my life, and I'm so grateful to still be here to help others. If my story resonates with you or someone you know—if my journey can give the hope and strength for even just one person to reach for the light; then I have fulfilled my ultimate mission. God bless!

Pirie's 5 Steps for Soul Success

1. Be Authentic! It's so important to be WHO YOU ARE! No one else on the planet has been given the talent, wisdom, drive, and personality that you have. You are one of a kind. Own it and be you. Everyone else is taken!

2. Be Courageous!
    Step out of your comfort zone so you can GROW. Go for what you want in life and don't be afraid to fail. When you start thinking out of the box, you spread your wings and fly. You've got what it takes. Just believe in yourself and your vision. Trust!

3. Don't put yourself UP FOR VOTE!
    Don't ask others what they think about your dreams or vision. Most people stay in their comfort zone and never try, so don't ask what others think about your dreams. They most likely will tell you that it's not possible or you should do it this way or that way, any other way but the one way you want. Listen to that still small voice inside of you and trust that voice. It's YOUR compass! Own it!

4. Have FAITH!
    Go beyond yourself. Believe in a Higher Power, God or whatever you believe in that is greater than yourself. Pray, meditate, ask for assistance. The Universe is conspiring FOR you! Never against you!

5. Be Disciplined in your thoughts and words!
    What you think and say creates action. Words create your reality! What you think is where you go. Keep negative thoughts and words out of your head, heart and Spirit!

CHAPTER 7

Owning Your Power & Getting What You Want

When we were finalizing the lineup for our first Soul Success Summit, my business partner Alisa mentioned a gal named Jaya Rose. "Jaya is exceptional! I don't know her personally but I've been following her for quite some time and she has a dramatic impact on spiritual business owners. We should ask her to speak." I had no idea who she was. Intrigued, I Googled her. I was not prepared for what I was about to see.

The first person to come up in my search engine was a porn star. My eyebrows raised, right before I realized that I was one letter off when I typed her name. That was a lesson we all must learn when "Googling" people. A simple letter can shift everything.

Happily, *our* Jaya Rose is another Jaya.

Jaya has a massive following and a killer Facebook group I now go to for guidance and daily reminders to stay compassionate and authentic. The first time I spoke with her, I felt the energy of our common mission to increase female consciousness. I knew she was our girl. When she finally spoke on our stage, there was a line of women waiting to ask questions and speak with her directly. She embodies self-confidence, love, and authenticity. And now, when I Google her name, THE REAL Jaya Rose comes up first: a dear friend who inspires me daily.

Jaya Rose

Have you ever had an experience in your life in which you can look back with your 20/20 vision and see the power and the transformation it created, but in the moment it felt like a total shit storm? That's what it felt like when I was going through my second divorce at age 30. I was in a repetitive cycle of constantly wanting more from men and always feeling disappointed.

"I wish he would pay more attention to me."

"I wish that he knew what I needed."

I had what I now call an addiction to disappointment.

It took me ten years and two failed marriages before I would realize it was my responsibility to actually ask for what I wanted. But I wouldn't wake up to that realization without a little kicking and screaming first.

Let me paint the picture for you: I had a good friend named Sarah who was a straight shooter. She said it like it was. When I went to her house one day, complaining about how my husband wasn't meeting my needs, blah blah blah, she dropped the mother of all truth bombs on me. She looked me square in the eyes and said, "What if this is actually about you, and not him?"

Say what? What I wanted was for her to feel bad for me and validate my victim feelings. But because she saw more in me than I saw in myself, she asked me to rise.

After feeling bad for myself and annoyed that she didn't validate my story, I went home and allowed the truth to settle in. I soon realized that some part of me was ready to tell a new story.

But as I said, it took some kicking and screaming.

What I did know immediately, though, is that I couldn't stand my part in the story anymore.

So I did what anyone would do. I called a couples counselor so he could tell my husband what he was doing wrong. Then I got up the gumption to tell my husband we needed to go to therapy and that I wasn't happy. He reluctantly said yes.

We went to see Louis Quimby to see if we were a good fit for his group couples therapy. Hint: We were not a good fit.

As we were sitting there, being assessed by this 70-year-old man who had been a family and relationship therapist for over 30 years, we were both afraid and had no idea what we were getting ourselves into.

I was eager to see the truth of what was going on, and my husband was eager to get the hell out of there. We started talking about what was happening in our relationship. Louis was so powerful and intimidating that everything I said felt like it was coming from a squeaky and afraid voice within. Kind of like when you go through customs and you are convinced you must be hiding something. Yah, he was *that* scary.

A big moment happened when, surprisingly, Louis looked at my husband and said, "You know you're with a really independent woman, right?"

"Um, what? I don't know what you're talking about," he said.

Louis said, "Let me ask you, how much would she get if you died? How much would she get from your life insurance?"

My husband replied, "I don't know. I think maybe $200,000."

Louis: "Okay, so you know she'd be fine without you, right? "

It was a fascinating and enlightening moment. As I look back, I think he was giving each of us our power back. We were both so locked in a co-dependent state; I felt like, if he's not okay, I'm not okay. And he felt like, if she's not okay, I'm not okay. And in that moment, it zapped us with a little bit of reality. We are two separate people.

Of course, there was a lot more to unlock.

At the end of the session, Louis said, "You're welcome to come to couples group therapy on Wednesdays at 5:30." My husband said, "No thanks."

My heart sank.

Louis saw through us, and turned to me and said, "You can come alone."

I made a bunch of ambivalent statements and we left.

Everything felt like a blur walking back to the car. I was about to make one of the biggest decisions of my life on that car ride home. I started by pleading with him to go to counseling with me. I begged him to grow with me. But he dug in his heels, saying he didn't need to go, and didn't understand why I thought we needed it.

In a moment of conceit, I put my head on the car window and started sobbing. I was mourning the loss of the woman I had been, who didn't ask for her needs, who would pick the same type of man again and again, incapable of understanding her value. I was mourning the loss of what would be the end of my marriage. Nothing from that moment forward would ever be the same.

I went to couples group therapy alone. Every Wednesday at 5:30, I went to a dark little therapy room with 3-4 other couples all fighting for their relationships, and what happened over the next six months would be the most powerful schooling of my life in self-love, functional relationships, and how to have a successful life. It was so much more than I had bargained for.

Once I wiped the tears (that rolled down my face for the first 3 sessions), I finally got it. I was there to (un)learn the me that created this reality, and to learn that the dysfunction and negative cycles I experienced in relationships was never really about them, it was always about me. It was about me and my very empty toolbox.

Louis gave me the tools to navigate a life by my design.

In the first or second session, Louis asked me, "How did you learn how to ask for your needs?" It took me a month to answer that question. When I finally did unlock the answer, so much truth came to the surface about why I wasn't ever getting my needs met, why I wasn't playing bigger in my life, and why I was failing miserably at marriage.

I realized that I was actually taught not to ask for my needs; that if I did ask, I was probably taking something away from someone else, that I should intuit what the other people needed, that I should be giving instead.

Growing up, I lived with a single mother and low-functioning sister. In the name of survival, my mother tried to tame down my especially decisive nature in order to give my sister room to ask for what she wanted. My mother meant well, but the strategy didn't work. At all. I'm still very decisive and my sister still has no idea what she wants out of life.

The freedom I felt from allowing that conditioning to fall away was powerful, and so was the unraveling that came next. I owned my power. I finally had permission to come home to the truth of who I am, and I learned some amazing life skills, too.

I toyed with the idea of staying in the marriage. It was sort of the last hurrah of the six-month therapy experience to decide what I was going to do. I remember going home to my husband after my Wednesday sessions, practicing the things I had learned. The marriage became my playground for trying out the new techniques I was learning in therapy.

I thought, what if I made a list of my requirements and shared them with him? What if I ask him to grow *with* me, instead of us growing apart?

I exhausted every idea and tool I had until it was clear that I couldn't learn anymore in the marriage, and that's when I decided I would leave.

At the time, my daughter, Becca, was eleven, and I knew it was my responsibility to show her what it looked like to be a strong woman who actually got her needs met and was willing to ask for what she wanted in life.

Later that year we moved to Portland, Oregon, and I began an adventure of practicing asking for my needs with real men. I knew that just diving into a new relationship would only result in me repeating the same cycle over and again.

So I dated. I dated for four years and, on every date, I held to the standards of what I desired in a partner.

And it was freaking hysterical.

They didn't know what was coming. I had a nice date with one guy. He asked me out again and then proceeded to stand me up.

I told him, "If you stand me up like that again, I won't date you anymore."

He did the same thing the next time we were supposed to go out.

Guess what I did? I honored my word and told him we're not going to date anymore.

He was shocked. He acted like he had no idea this was coming and that this was the biggest tragedy of his life. And I thought, wow, this is what is available for women when we don't ask for what we need, when we don't show up for ourselves, when we don't value ourselves.

The big lesson I learned through all of the dating was that there is no guarantee that we get what we want. That became very clear.

I strengthened my "asking for what I want" muscle and got super clear on how to ask both men and the Universe to give to me! This is the single most powerful thing I have ever done.

I met my third husband, Jonathan, after four years of being single and dating. He is amazing and we have the relationship I've always wanted. He lives up to what I always wanted, because from the beginning, I said what I wanted. We have a beautiful relationship and have been married for seven years *and* we have a beautiful daughter, Ava, who is 6.

The ability to stand in my truth and know who I am at the core set me on a mission to help other people do the same thing. I feel a deep call to help other women rise, too. I realized that if I was experiencing these self-sabotaging patterns, many other women were, too.

Now, thirteen years after my time in therapy with Louis, I followed the call to help others and have a popular online brand called *She Rise,* which empowers women all over the world to own their power, speak their truth, and make money doing what they love! I look back at the experience in that dark therapy office and see that it was a spark.

It was the catalyst for filling my "toolbox" and changing my patterns to have a healthy relationship and to have another shot at having a family. I have broken free from the stigma of being a young, un-educated single mother, and I get to choose my life, and I get to help other people do the same thing.

Here's what I want to ask you: What would your life look like if you allowed yourself to ask for what you really wanted, to step into a more powerful version of yourself and release the need to please other people and play small?

There is a next-level version of you that is just waiting for permission to emerge. There is a part of you who desires more.

Here is a three-step process I use when I have new desires.

Step One:

Ask yourself what you desire, and get honest. Be clear and provide as much detail as possible. If you feel resistance, allow it to rise within you. Breathe. Talk through it, or journal until it passes. Make sure that you can feel into the desire with a clear focus, void of negative self-talk or resistance.

Step Two:

Ask yourself what feelings you will feel when this desire becomes real? Name the feelings. What do you need to shift in your life to be in those feelings more often? Shift those things and focus on your desired feelings as if you were holding a plank. I call this a Spiritual Plank.

Side note: This phase can take a while, as it did for me while I shifted my beliefs and "practiced" dating.

Step Three:

Notice the places in your life that validate that your desire is coming true. Be a crazy person and celebrate every small victory! Interpret any plot twists that come up as opportunities to simply redirect you toward your desire. Create your own evidence that things are changing in your favor. When you honor the little things, you expand your capacity to receive and hold the bigger things.

And now you are now an actual magnet to your desire!

I hope you take from my story the knowledge that you are so incredibly valuable. That you, your voice, and your ability to ask for what you really want in life, are the most powerful things you have, and that when you amplify them, you become a champion of possibility for others.

There is so much more possible for our lives than we could ever imagine, and this story is just a small glimpse into how I opened up to a greater possibility in my life. I hope it inspires you to do the same thing in your own life.

When one woman takes responsibility for her life and chooses a new path, she paves the way for others to do the same.

I believe we create the majority of our own limitations, and that when we free ourselves from them and rise, we give opportunity for others to rise with us, and this my friend, is our great collective purpose. To rise together.

My final wish for you is that you always remember: When you move, everything moves.

Relationships

*"If only you could sense how important you are
to the lives of those you meet; how important
you can be to people you may never even dream of.
There is something about yourself that you leave
at every meeting with another person."*
– Fred Rogers

Relationships are one of the most important aspects of being human. As I continue to work on my Soul Success, I am continually reminded that we are all connected. There was a period in my life that I felt disconnected from others. I felt like I couldn't understand others, and they couldn't understand me. In spirituality, non-dualism is a level of consciousness to remind us that we are universally connected. Dualism tells us that we are separate from God while non-dualism tells us that we are all a part of God. We are all one. This is why we feel empty when we isolate ourselves from others.

It wasn't until I learned the importance of relationships and how to be a genuine friend that I was able to fill the void buried deep inside of me. Connecting with others by sharing your story and taking a stand is a powerful way to nourish your soul and find alignment. But always remember, that the greatest relationship you will ever have is the one you have with yourself. When you learn to love and nourish your soul, the relationships you have with others will follow.

CHAPTER 8

Finding Enough

As I remember, it all started with an invitation for coffee. Leah was visiting Sun Valley and wanted to connect about what I was doing in my business. From what I knew, she was a rock star film producer and entrepreneur. So we met for coffee and she started telling me about a film she was screening in our town based on the life of her grandmother, "Big Sonia," one of the last living holocaust survivors.

When I asked Leah why she felt inspired to create this film, she said, "The effects of the Holocaust are still playing a role today. The trauma passed down from generation to generation still needs awareness. All of our grandparents experienced trauma during the war. Our parents were too close to it to do anything about it. And now our generation actually has the tools to do something about it. This is my duty not just to my Grandma, but to human-kind, to spread the mission of kindness and compassion."

Before that conversation, I hadn't put much thought into the significant trauma that is passed down through epigenetics. My first thought was that Big Sonia had stories to tell! And Leah was taking something so dark and turning into a vehicle to educate, inspire, and impact others. Since that first coffee date, I have come to know and love both Sonia and Leah.

Leah Warshawski

My grandmother, Sonia, is 4'8" and she can barely see over the steering wheel of her giant, pink Buick. At 94, she still goes into work every day at her late husband's tailor shop in the corner of a dead mall in suburban Kansas City. She's a self-proclaimed fashion expert, and you can see her lipstick a mile away. She swears animal prints will never go out of style. She's a local celebrity, a role-model, and a Holocaust survivor.

Sonia spent her teenage years in some of the most notorious and horrific concentration camps during WWII. She watched her mother walk to the gas chamber and watched countless people commit suicide because daily life was too painful. She escaped death and "selections" countless times, and on the day of liberation, Sonia was accidentally shot through the chest. Miraculously, she survived.

She met her husband, John, in a displacement camp after the War and they were sent to Kansas City to start a new life. They had to teach themselves English. My father and his sisters remember hearing a lot of things that kids aren't supposed to hear growing up. The Holocaust was, and still is, a dark cloud that hangs over families and generations, and it never goes away.

John died when I was young, and Sonia reluctantly took over the shop. Even though she doesn't sew, John's Tailoring has a steady stream of customers who show up just to spend time with Sonia and sit on her iconic, leopard-print loveseat.

She's one of the only Holocaust survivors in the Kansas City area who speaks publicly about her wartime experience to anyone who will listen. A quick trip to drop off tailoring can easily turn into a day-long pilgrimage with meals provided by Sonia, stories, Yiddish partisan songs and book recommendations. It's an *experience* and one that I couldn't resist as a filmmaker.

When Sonia turned 84 in 2010, my husband and I set out to make a short film about *John's Tailoring* and all of the fascinating customers who come in for their own redemption. It's hard to believe that initially we planned to make a film about a Holocaust survivor without focusing on the Holocaust. We learned quickly that this was impossible. We spent more time filming in the shop and followed Sonia on speaking engagements at schools and prisons.

We interviewed my family about what it was like growing up in the shadow of so much trauma, and it felt like we were peeling back layers of an onion. Tears, laughter, tragedy, and more tears. Before we knew it, our short film turned into a 93-minute feature, and the smallest woman I knew became the star of our movie, *Big Sonia*. A project we intended to be comical and detached became very heavy and personal. I didn't understand all of the implications and I didn't predict that *Big Sonia* would take a decade to produce and distribute.

Growing up as a member of the *Third Generation*, a grandchild of Holocaust survivors, continues to have a profound impact on every aspect of my life, but I'm just now, at 41 years old, beginning to understand all of the implications and nuances that show up when I least expect them. Children and grandchildren of survivors who I've met in the last ten years have echoed similar feelings and experiences.

- For most of my life, I've struggled to feel like I'm *enough*. Smart enough, skinny enough, healthy enough, pretty enough, successful enough—you name it, I'm always searching for more and underwhelmed by my achievements.
- Freelance work is the only kind of work I can do. I value freedom and mobility above all else. Confined spaces or too many rules cause panic.
- I'm always thinking about an Exit Strategy and a plan B—always creating options in work and relationships.
- Almost everyone in my family has food issues: deeply engrained food rules, and obsessive/manic behavior around food.

Yet despite those challenges and negativity, I have "gifts" handed down from my ancestors that are impossible to ignore:

- Appreciation and reverence for nature and animals
- Resilience and perseverance
- Strong work ethic
- Ability and interest in learning other languages

In 2017, after six years of working on *Big Sonia,* and spending more time with my grandmother (and extended family) than I ever bargained for, I gave a TEDx Talk entitled *How Do You Cope With the Trauma You Didn't Experience?* It was my way of beginning to unpack some of the issues I had kept private for so long: anxiety, self-criticism, negative body image, issues around food, and never feeling like I was enough. Giving the talk was nerve-wracking and also therapeutic because it helped me think through a compelling way to present the topic. But it was just the tip of the iceberg.

I spent the next two years on the road presenting *Big Sonia* at film festivals, community screenings, theaters, and in Congress. I spoke about my family's trauma and listened to hundreds of stories from people who related our film to trauma in their own lives. People told me stories about rape, suicide, war, discrimination, bullying, and I tried to be a compassionate sounding board. In many cases people were telling secrets they had never divulged.

In addition to dealing with my own issues and insecurities, the stories I was entrusted with were piling up and feeling more like a burden than a gift. For a private person who doesn't like to talk about herself, promoting a personal film is a complicated challenge.

While the film continued to succeed and win festivals and accolades, I was spiraling deeper into self-hatred and unhappiness. I put my well-being on hold. It was more important to me that the film succeed and have praise from my family—success at any cost—because I felt immense pressure on every level, personal, professional, and cultural. After what Sonia survived, her story deserved to be told. And seen.

After everything Sonia endured, I didn't want to seem weak or incapable of doing my job. I plowed through events and screenings in every corner of the country and got used to being uncomfortable and unhealthy. If you've spent a lot of time alone on the road (especially women), you understand that it's not easy to find healthy food or a gym, and that barricading your hotel room door and sleeping on top of the covers is totally normal in many small towns.

Then one day, toward the end of the two-year road tour, I was driving from Kansas City to St. Louis to give a presentation at my former high school. I was an over-achiever in high school but, like many teenagers, I was hiding much pain and shame that I had no idea how to process. All of those feelings came back to me as I was driving on the highway, and I had an alarming thought. If I crashed the car and injured myself, I could get out of this commitment.

It was a defining moment for me, to realize that I had given myself over completely to the project while talking about trauma and the Holocaust every day. It was time for me to get back to what brought me joy. Everything felt like duty, obligation, and responsibility. I was miserable. It was time to set better boundaries for health and sanity, and to be an active participant in my own life-design versus passively accepting what other people were planning for me. I needed to look to Sonia as a model. After the War, Sonia could have chosen silence and faded into obscurity, but she chose to speak out as a witness, start a business, and grow a family.

Sonia says she "stays busy to keep the dark parts away," and in this way, we're similar. She still goes into work six days a week because in down time her trauma comes back like a flood. I was great at masking everything with work and over-achieving, but Sonia also taught me that every day is precious. She reminds me what true resilience looks like. She took a horrific experience and created a life filled with meaning and exponential impact. How many 94-year-olds do you know who get a standing ovation when they walk into a middle school cafeteria? How many grandmothers have a day named after them (The annual *Big Sonia Day* in Kansas City)?

We have a complicated relationship built upon mutual respect, admiration, guilt, obligation, joy, and pain. My grandmother can drink more than I can, she can stay up later than I can, and she has more friends than I do. She can make me feel awesome and horrible in the same sentence. She thinks I'm selfish for not wanting kids. She is hurtful and delightful. Excited and depressed. She's a role-model, an icon, and the ultimate diva. She is me, and I am her. And I am grateful.

When all of the Holocaust survivors are gone, who will tell their stories? Who will care? It's one of the reasons we're still working so hard on impact and education for *Big Sonia*. Making films is my job, but it's not my *life*. I love my family, but I've also learned how toxic some family relationships can be. At the end of the day, as long as I keep perspective and set my own boundaries, I'm confident that Sonia is proud of me and "her film," as she lovingly calls it.

***

Epilogue:
We premiered *Big Sonia* one day after the Election in 2016 and we haven't stopped since. After more than seventy-five film festivals, a theatrical release, Academy Awards qualification, and more than two hundred community screenings, we're still working hard to spread the #SoniaEffect. Making and distributing films is not for the faint of heart, but what keeps me going is the reactions I see from teenagers. In our current world where anti-Semitism and hate crimes are on the rise, people are looking for models of resilience, unity, empathy, and hope. *Big Sonia* has become our way to open

up important and difficult conversations, and the project has become our beacon of hope when the world around us doesn't seem to make sense. There are currently only twelve states that mandate Holocaust education in classrooms, and we're working hard to change that. We believe there has never been a more important time for this film, its themes, and for Sonia herself. And it looks like she may just outlive us all.

My advice to you: Surround yourself with people who inspire, encourage, and challenge you. Downsize personal relationships that stem from obligation and duty and focus on relationships that are reciprocal. Every time I do this, I feel like a weight is lifted and it allows me to focus on meaningful and healthy relationships instead of toxic ones. People who exhaust you or don't treat you with respect don't deserve your time and energy. Be humble and curious about the world and everyone you meet. I feel like we grow as humans by being good listeners and really *hearing* what people are going through. Sonia says, "Put love in your heart." Isn't that the perfect way to approach everyone and everything you meet?

Justice. Nature. Education. Climate Protection. Fresh Air. Personal Freedom. Authenticity. My mission is to impact people's lives in a memorable and positive way—through the films and content I create, and by being a kind, compassionate and resilient person. To inspire people to live their best and most authentic lives by living MY best life. I want to give more than I take, and I want to create life-changing experiences for people. Since I'm choosing not to have kids, my legacy will be the impact I make on others and I'm determined to do the best I can with what I've been given.

"Soul Success" is knowing that you're "enough" and celebrating whatever makes you uniquely *you*. It's knowing and enforcing your own boundaries and a willingness to be vulnerable. It's about forgiving yourself and learning from every challenge. Soul Success is designing your future with intent and savoring the journey.

Leah's 5 Steps to Soul Success

1. Record / document your family history while your parents and grandparents are still alive. Every family has legends, myths, and stories that are passed down between generations. Before it's too late, record stories on camera or via audio interviews; you'll be amazed what happens when you ask specific questions.

2. Do more of what you enjoy and less of what you don't. After two years on the road promoting our film (giving all of my energy to other people), I needed to regain control of my schedule and sanity. Make a list of the things that bring you joy and carve out time every day to do something on that list. This should be non-negotiable time.

3. Find a mentor and be a mentor. We all need advice and guidance during the journey, and it feels good to be able to guide others as well.

4. Support Holocaust education in classrooms. Support policy initiatives. You can learn more on our website, www.bigsonia.com.

CHAPTER 9

Lessons from Children

They say you shouldn't become friends with your clients. I get that. When you get too close to the ones you work with, boundaries can get fuzzy. My business is different. Because working with me is a journey of uncovering layers, building trust, and growth, my clients become some of my best friends. Jaime is no exception. Upon meeting her, it was love at first sight. We quickly learned that we share similar values in spirituality, family, health, and relationships.

I believe that when building relationships, loyalty and integrity should be two of the first things to look at and those are two of the first words I would use to describe Jaime. We are co-captains in a fighter jet: sharing common values and a mission to change the way people see the world.

We live in Sun Valley, a small ski resort town (like a few of the other authors in this book). Jaime has become famous in our town for working magic on children and parents as a social learning specialist. I believe that in today's world, there are far too many diagnoses (and misdiagnoses, for that matter). Knowing what might be wrong with ourselves or our kids is often a puzzle; we are constantly trying to learn how to put the pieces together.

The world today is more complicated than ever. With that, we are stressed out, overwhelmed, and pressured by society's standards to fit in a box. Jaime has been a sounding board for our community on how to solve life's puzzle in the social world. She leaves her community with practical tools on how to build relationships as well as enhance learning and creativity.

Jaime Rivetts

I was watching the news with my almost two-year-old daughter when a report came in about yet another school shooting. Kids were walking into schools and shooting other kids. It just keeps happening over and over again. It's a part of our culture. I immediately wept and tried to hide my tears from my daughter. I was pregnant at the time, and I remember thinking there are mothers right now who are grieving the loss of their child right after sending them to school for the day. How could I be a mother and not do anything about this? What will happen when my girls are old enough to go to school? Schools should be the safest place for your child. Instead school shootings are becoming a threat to children.

In 2019, out of forty-six weeks, there were forty-five school shootings. That fact is astounding and appalling. We need to stop arguing over solutions and start making changes now. We sure as hell can't wait for another politician to try and fix gun control. Or wait for someone to start yelling, "Don't take away my 2nd Amendment rights!" Last time I checked, that didn't include allowing guns in schools. No one was finding solutions and everyone was getting in their own way. The only people that seemed to be making progress on the issue were the children involved in the shootings. School shootings were a complex situation that needed multiple solutions.

The profile of most of the school shooters is the same. These young adults or adolescents are usually bullied, socially isolated loners, with mental health challenges. These were fixable problems. As a mother and an educator, I saw only solutions. These kids need support understanding the complex social world and navigating their relationships. They need help finding the right support if they are struggling with a mental health challenge.

I know how hard it is to parent. We can't be expected to do everything and do it well. I have a background in behavior and I can't tell you how many times I've thrown my hands in the air with my three-year old and said, "I have no idea what to do!" I have a Master's degree in education and fifteen years of experience teaching children, adolescents, and adults about the social world, and I still don't have any idea what I'm doing? So I can't imagine where to begin supporting a child that has special needs without any background on navigating the complexity of the social world. Hence my mission. I am developing products, programs, and courses that will help support others with the social world and help parents teach the complexities of the social world to their children. We have to do better and we can do better for our children. I have made this my mission and my passion behind my work.

Relationships are the most important thing in your life—relationships with yourself, your significant other, your family members, your children, your co-workers, your friends. This is the foundation of everything that you do in life. So if you want to be a good mom, business owner, friend, wife, or even an entrepreneur, start with understanding the complexities of your relationships.

When Megan asked me to write for her book, so many thoughts ran through my head. Relationships are a vast topic. There are so many things I could talk about that I find valuable. Then I sat down and I thought about it. What do parents really need to know to support their children? How can I help other parents support their children's relationships? I had been helping people with their relationships for fifteen years; surely I had some good advice for them. As a mom, these lessons have taken a whole new shape and meaning to me. Not only are they relative to my clients but they have been very helpful in parenting my own children. Who knew that all these years I was really preparing myself for what to do with my own children?

The Boy Who Asked "Why Hasn't Anyone Told Me This Before?"

I had been working with an eighth-grade boy for almost a year when we had a huge breakthrough. We went to the grocery store to make observations of what others were doing in order to better understand the social world. We had been talking about figuring out what we were supposed to do in social situations for months. When they're ready for it, I find it easiest to practice this skill when I go into the community with my clients. Then we can work in real life situations and create "social autopsies." This basically means pulling apart the social context and scenario and breaking it into chunks you can understand and interpret so you know what to do. Most of my students know what an autopsy entails, and they like the analogy of pulling something apart to understand it better. Our plan was simple: Select something at the grocery store and then stand in line to pay for it.

Throughout scenarios like this, things come up that seem simple to you and me but are often complicated for others. My client kept bumping into others because he wasn't aware of his body in space. We talked about how to navigate the aisles in the grocery store. You had to look ahead and anticipate other people's moves.

He said he just did his best not to walk into others but hadn't realized how much he needed to think about where he was walking. When we were standing in line waiting to pay for our food, he decided to be friendly and strike up a conversation with someone else in line. He proceeded to be "overly friendly" and asked the other person in line what they thought about the food they were buying and how often they came into the store? Then he went into detail about his sushi and the different types of fish he likes, where they come from in the ocean, and how much soy he likes to use when he eats sushi.

The person he was talking to looked at him strangely and slowly backed away. My client didn't pick up on any of this. He kept talking and tried really hard to use a very friendly tone.

Everyone in line, including the cashier, looked at him strangely. My lesson was backfiring on me. For months I had been working with him on what to ask people when he talked to them, and it was important to him to come across as friendly. The problem is that if you start talking to someone in the grocery store line like you know them, it doesn't quite come off as friendly. I decided to wait until we got back to my office to do the social autopsy.

When we got back to the office, I asked how he thought everything went.

"Great!" he said. "I think I came across as really friendly. I didn't have my money lined up when I paid for my sushi, but other than that I nailed it!"

He may have been socially unaware, but his motives were genuine. Why had things unfolded this way for him? No one had taught him the difference between friendly and creepy. How could I teach him that the complexities of our social interactions depend on the level of our understanding and relationships with that person. Where did I start to help him understand?

I asked what kind of thoughts the woman he approached in line might have had about him during their chat. He said that she thought he was a friendly person. I said "Nope, not even close." After a long discussion, he finally realized that he didn't know that lady in line at all, and that he took the conversation too far. He also realized that he missed her body language as well as the nonverbal clues others were giving him.

In short, the lady in line and those around him had strange thoughts about him.

He looked at me, and said, "Why hasn't anyone ever taught me this before? I had no idea people had thoughts about me and that my whole life I was giving other people weird thoughts."

I was almost laughing with joy. He was mystified and enlightened.

And he was terrified. We talked about impressions, and who you talk to, and what you talk about. We spent months dissecting that single situation in the grocery store.

Today, that boy is thriving in college, and the last I heard he had a lot of friends.

Here is my golden nugget of advice: Teach your kids everything in the social world. And teach them even when they might be too young to pick up on things. Talk to them out loud about what other people might be thinking and feeling. When I take my three-year-old daughter to someone's house for dinner, I might say, "Maeve, can you say hi to everyone in the room, please?"

Then I whisper to her that everyone will think she's friendly and may want to play with her. Then I proceed to tell her how to introduce herself and WHY it's important. THINK OUT LOUD WITH YOUR KIDS WHEN YOU ARE PARENTING. Tell them what runs through your heads in social situations when you make a decision or interact with someone else. We often prompt kids what *not* to do without telling them *why*.

I often hear parents tell their children "Get down!" "Don't do that!" or "Stop it!" but not WHY they need to stop doing all of those things. Tell kids this is what could happen if you don't stop, or this is what people might think about you if you keep doing this. My three-year-old is a comedian and she loves attention from others. She is my performer. Lately she thinks showing other people her cute booty is appropriate in a social situation. I have probably created this problem because I tell her things like, "What a cute booty!"

I have had extensive talks with her that she is only allowed to do that booty shake at home with FAMILY. The other day she was doing it at our house but non-family members were also present. I suspect I may have to reinforce this point as she gets older.

The eighth-grade boy at the grocery store didn't know why he needed to stop talking to the woman in line. He thought that *talking* equaled *friendly* and, clearly, she wanted to hear all about the different types of fish you could eat that was safe for sushi, didn't she?

The Boy Who Said, "No One Likes Me and I Don't Know Why"

My mentor was discussing one of our most needy and tricky clients with the staff. She was discussing who would work with this elementary-aged boy who had blown out of several schools and was giving his parents a full-on run for their money. I tried to keep a low profile in the meeting, but I just knew she was going to ask me.

She finally turned to me and said, "Jaime I would like you to work with him. It will be one of the most challenging students you ever work with, but you'll learn more in a few months with him than you will in years working with other clients."

I had been working in the field in private practice for only a little over a year. Why would she pick one of the least qualified therapists to work with the most challenging client?

She assured me she wouldn't send me into the sessions unprepared, and she broke down what to do and how to do it. She told me to start simple. Let him pick what he wants to do but then ask to have a say in the lesson as well. Make it visual, structured, and use small chunks of language. The family is a 10, she told me, and was willing to listen to any suggestions.

I had insomnia for days leading up to our first session. I called my mother for advice.

"Well, there's a reason your mentor picked you to work with this client," she said. "She thinks you can do it, and thinks you'll learn a lot from the experience."

My mother would tell me to climb Mt. Everest even if I was asthmatic and recovering from a lung transplant. She believed I was capable of anything I put my mind to.

The day the session arrived, I had notes, note cards, sticky notes, markers, stickers, pencils (sharpened and unsharpened), Kleenex, games, stuffed animals, bottles of water, and hope that I was prepared for anything. My goal, simple enough, was my mentor's goal for me: to stay in the room with the boy for fifty minutes without incident.

It was anything but simple. He was simply delightful when I met him. Full of joy, handsome, and outgoing. I created a simple visual plan on the board and allowed him to have a say in what he wanted to do with me. Things went well for the first ten minutes, then twenty minutes. The next minute he told me that no one liked him and he didn't know why. And then was storming around the room threatening to explode. He was angry for the rest of the lesson but he didn't leave the room.

Over the next few months, the boy erupted similarly over what appeared to me to be the smallest problems. My only goal through these sessions was my original goal: keep him calm and in the room with me for fifty minutes. If he didn't storm out of the room and go to his mother in the waiting room, we considered the session a success. I spent almost an entire school year working with him one-on-one, merely getting him to tolerate sharing space with another human being who was asking him to do things for almost an hour.

Through it all, I HAD NO IDEA WHAT I WAS DOING AND I DIDN'T THINK IT WAS WORKING. I constantly consulted with my mentor and his mother. His mother, a retired palliative care nurse, had adopted him. She cared for those who were sick and dying for a living. She was an absolute saint.

She went on to tell me how she wasn't able to naturally conceive so she had adopted him and had no idea where his history of behaviors came from. The universe could not have picked a more loving and patient human being to raise this boy. She repeatedly told me she had no idea what she was doing, but she was sure she was doing everything wrong. I was the therapist, and I didn't know what to say to her or what to do. I was supposed to be the expert.

I fell in love with the boy and this family—fast and hard. I stayed up late at night researching lesson ideas, reading books from experts who specialized in educating and parenting the most challenging kids, and I worried over and over again that I didn't know what I was doing.

I went to his birthday party to support the family and did school observations to help his teachers. The family bought me the Christmas gifts. We supported one another. His mother cried on my shoulder and celebrated with me when he made it through his birthday party without threatening to hurt anyone. I felt lost and hopeless at times, but I just kept telling myself the family needed my help, and so I forged on. My mentor encouraged me to continue working with him, and there was no way I was giving him up to work with anyone else. If I was sick for a session, he didn't come to the clinic and work with anyone else. One day he told me that he called the clinic the *FBI*.

When I asked if that was a good thing, he told me it stood for the flexible brain institute.

One day, after many months of therapy, I finally realized I could put him in a group with another boy. He could work with another peer! We were moving on up in the therapy world. Now he had to think about me and another person.

The first few months were an absolute disaster. He left the therapy room all the time and told me, through clenched teeth, that no one liked him and that he didn't like anyone else. By disaster I mean shit flew across the room. At one point he got so mad at me for what I was asking him to do he left the room and picked up a plastic basketball hoop to throw at me. Just before he was about to launch it at me, I told him if he threw it at me he wouldn't be allowed to come back to the clinic. He threw it, anyway. Then he burst into tears, and so did his mother who was standing on the side lines. I went into the bathroom and cried in a stall.

I had failed him. I had pushed him too hard and he tried to hurt me. That was the quickest way to get kicked out of the clinic.

I talked my mentor into letting him come back with a strict contract and boundaries.

The boy apologized profusely and told me he couldn't live without our weekly lessons. I was making a difference, even though it didn't seem like it. Eventually, he learned to manage his emotions and think about others more. He went from a small group to a bigger group and he started to make a real effort to make other people happy. He started to make a few friends and have successful play dates.

I worked with him for years. He was, and always will be, the MOST REWARDING CLIENT I EVER HAD. I can't tell you how many times a day I looked at my husband and said, "I have no idea what to do with this child."

Parenting and relationships can be daunting and confusing. Reach out to others. Ask for help. Don't give up. Things will change and get better. IT'S OKAY TO NOT KNOW WHAT TO DO.

A few years later when I moved from California to be with family in Idaho, he cried on my shoulder but told me he'd be okay working with someone else. He understood that I needed to be with my family. His mother thanked me over and over again. He gave me a small statue of a woman helping a child. He told me it represented our relationship.

I treasured this gift until it broke one day. Two years after I moved to Idaho, he died on a hiking trip in the backcountry. His appendix burst and he was in too remote of a location to get to a hospital in time. He was fifteen years old. I think about him all the time. He reminds me to never give up on anyone. He reminds me that people can change. He reminds me that sometimes when we are angry, we say things we don't mean. He reminds me to give people second chances. But most of all, he reminds me that SOMETIMES WE DON'T KNOW WHAT TO DO BUT WE WILL FIND A WAY.

The Girl Who Said, "If I Wear Black, Other People Will Leave Me Alone"

She was in middle school when I met her, and when I say that she wore all black, I mean all black: black make-up, black hair, black eyeliner and black clothes. She had her hair parted down the middle of her face so that only part of her face was showing. She hid at home, staying in her room for hours at a time. She hid at school. She slunk along the hallways and kept to herself.

She wasn't letting anyone in.

I would be a rich woman if someone paid me every time a teenager told me, "I don't care what others think." And she said it all the time.

After fifteen years of working with teens, I can assure you that they ALL CARE. They just don't always know how to show it, or how to react when others don't seem to care about them. It's an excuse to hide behind, and it's a silent cry for help if you know what to listen for.

It took me months to crack her brash and rude exterior.

I began by asking her why she bothered showering every day if she didn't care what others thought of her. She had an answer for everything, though, and she tried her best to loop herself back to her safe place. She showered because she liked to shower, not because she cared what others thought. She admitted that she wore all black so others would leave her alone. Her tactics were working: She had no friends.

It was easier to say you didn't care and you could be whoever you wanted to be. The truth is that all kids care what others think of them, and they sometimes need help understanding how they can become a likeable person after so much social rejection.

Then one day she broke. I cracked the uncrackable exterior. She burst into tears and told me she wanted friends, and maybe even a boyfriend someday. She just didn't know how to do it. Others had bullied and picked on her and it was easier to become this dark, looming person than get them to stop. If she could become invisible and repel others, then she was safe. Other kids would leave her alone. But they left her alone too much and she was lonely. She was tired of hiding in her room on the weekends and binge-watching dark drama series for teens. She admitted that she wanted people to like her, but she needed help.

I had her in the right place. The hard part was over, the easy part was teaching her what to do. We started with clothing and outward appearance. She started to pull her hair back and tuck it behind her ear so people could see her beautiful face. She let me do a total wardrobe makeover. The only two colors other than grey and black she would allow in her wardrobe were purple and pink. We researched stores kids her age liked to shop at. We went to Forever 21, and she reinvented herself.

She scaled back on the makeup and started wearing brighter colors. I explained and re-explained that people would start to see her as approachable and maybe even friendly with these shifts. When I saw her at school she was still looking down or away, so I told her she had to start making EYE CONTACT with others and giving them a slight smile. A week later she burst into my office and said, "IT WORKED! OTHER PEOPLE ARE TALKING TO ME AND SMILING AT ME!" She said walking down the halls to school didn't seem so frightening anymore and people were actually reciprocating with smiles and hellos.

I fell out of my chair and said, "NO WAY! THERE ARE NICE PEOPLE IN THE WORLD?"

She found a circle of friends and got invited to dances, houses, and the movies. Boys started to notice her, and eventually she had a serious boyfriend. Then the weekly discussions shifted to the do's and don'ts of dating and more intricate issues with male-female relationships. Her parents' worries shifted to worrying about her falling in love with the wrong guy. Where we started was so different than where we ended up, and that was a good place to be. I often misunderstand my three-year old daughter's behavior. I call her a *threenager* because there are ups and downs and a lot of drama.

There are so many golden nuggets with this story I don't know where to start. You can't ever give up on someone. There might be a reason someone is doing what they are doing. You might think you understand someone else, but you could be DEAD WRONG. This teenage girl dressed in black was dying to connect positively with others, but it wasn't the message she was sending. Fortunately, her parents sought help. If I had assumed like everyone else that she wanted to be left alone then imagine where she might still be?

Nuggets of gold:

1. *TEACH YOUR KIDS EVERYTHING. BY EVERYTHING I MEAN THINK OUT LOUD SO THEY UNDERSTAND WHAT TO DO. DON'T ASSUME THEY UNDERSTAND, OR THAT THEY WILL EVENTUALLY LEARN IT. TEACH THEM TO BE KIND AND FRIENDLY TO PEOPLE AND WHY IT'S IMPORTANT. ONCE WE START TEACHING KIDS THE "WHY" BEHIND WHAT WE DO, THEN THINGS START TO CHANGE.*

2. *SOMETIMES WE DON'T KNOW WHAT TO DO AND WE FIND OUR WAY. DON'T GIVE UP. I HAVE GIVE-UP MOMENTS ALL THE TIME WITH CLIENTS AND EVEN WITH MY OWN CHILDREN. ASK FOR HELP. TAKE BREAKS. I AM*

SO GLAD I DIDN'T GIVE UP ON THE HARDEST CLIENT I HAVE EVER WORKED WITH BECAUSE HE MADE ME A BETTER PERSON, A BETTER MOM AND A BETTER THERAPIST.

3. *BE CAREFUL ABOUT YOUR JUDGMENT. OTHER PEOPLE MIGHT BE HURTING INSIDE AND SENDING YOU THE WRONG MESSAGE. TAKE THE TIME TO GET TO KNOW SOMEONE AND PEEL AWAY THE LAYERS THAT MAKE THEM UNIQUE. YOU MIGHT BE ABLE TO HELP THEM AND MAKE A BIG DIFFERENCE IN THEIR LIFE.*

CHAPTER 10

Shakti

Barbara embodies shakti—divine feminine strength and leadership. I met her a few years ago after she applied to speak at the Soul Success Summit. She is an author, TEDx speaker, and social psychologist. And absolutely stunning.

Since first connecting, Barbara has always been among the first to stand up in our online community and celebrate the accomplishments of others. She is strong, bold, and beautiful. She has won multiple awards for female leadership in her country. Barbara is recognized as being one of the most influential women in Namibia.

Barbara Kamba-Nyathi

The rollercoaster journey of my becoming began in November of 2009 when I was diagnosed with cervical cancer. I did not see this coming; nature was playing a cruel joke on me. Early that year I had started volunteering at the Cancer Association of Namibia and I was providing psychotherapy to patients and survivors. I was the one on the other side. I was not one of them. To be diagnosed with cancer was a huge insult to my essence. I refused to accept it, and embarked on a prayer for my hair, because it was important that I did not lose my hair during this ordeal. I could not afford to look like them. This was ridiculous, of course—because I have alopecia. I already had bald patches on my head which I skillfully hid with my beautiful locks from the world. I did not lose my hair then, but now I am bald and know that it's okay to be one of them. We are, after all, a sisterhood on a journey together, for each other.

As it turns out, cancer was my saving grace. Without it I would have not had the deeper understanding and appreciation of my body that I now have, and I would have most likely died from endometriosis. The surgical operation for cancer and the ultrasound scan following the diagnosis led to the discovery of the endometriosis, which had advanced to stage four. It was the commencement of a challenging and tumultuous period. I barely had time to process all this information and its implications. The focus was about saving my life and the doctors preserving what they could. From November 2009 to April 2018, I bagged fourteen surgical operations, deafness and a swollen pituitary gland before getting the autoimmune disease properly diagnosed.

But the challenges did not end there. I was also abused, cheated on, divorced, and had a hysterectomy.

I have since come to the conclusion that the cancer and endometriosis were the universe's effort to make sure that I never became a mother. I say this not out of anger or bitterness, but as a fact of life. When I was sixteen years old, a significant male in my life sexually harassed me. The incident broke my heart. I vowed I would never be a parent, simply to ensure that no child of mine would be subjected to what I went through. Those who were supposed to protect and comfort me in that time of need rejected me and blamed me for what had happened. In that moment, I lost all faith in parenting. Because I had put promise out to the universe, I believe it made sure that my cervix and uterus were so damaged I would not be able to procreate, ever. The many surgical operations resulted in the necessity for a hysterectomy. On the bright side, I do not menstruate anymore, though I do experience the *glow moments*, which I adamantly refuse to call hot flushes. I don't do hot flushes. I glow.

One day, in July of 2012, I woke up deaf. I went to see an ear, nose, and throat specialist who ordered an MRI scan of my brain. It turned out there was nothing wrong with my ears but the scan revealed that I had a swollen pituitary gland. The doctor panicked and wanted to send me to a neurosurgeon, but that is where I drew the line with surgery. No one in this lifetime was going to cut into my head. I resisted the suggestion until the poor doctor gave up. It's bad enough that I was getting operated on twice a year because of the other conditions. But it helped explain the hint of crazy and crankiness that I had, and that was my first lesson in learning to accept that I was different. Thankfully, my hearing returned in nine months.

The temporary deafness, however, sent my ex into a frenzy.

When the cheating started, my husband became very abusive emotionally and verbally. The man could spew such vile words from his mouth that I was traumatized for months on end. He changed from being my friend and rock to a monster I couldn't stand. The cat came out of the bag when he "cheated" on one of his hoes. She got angry and told me everything. I was so hurt and broken, I knew at that moment I would divorce him. What I did not know was how long it would take me to actually do it. Between July 2015 and May 2017, so much happened that getting a divorce took a backseat to all of the other items on my to-do list. My mother passed away, I had a hysterectomy, my body went through serious changes. It was a nightmare. During all this time, my husband was revealing astounding levels of asshole.

When I couldn't take it anymore, I filed for divorce. Four months later, our marriage was dissipated, and I began a new chapter.

Obstacles

I remember being so very angry that I was terrified of myself. I was angry with my parents for having me. I was angry with God. I questioned His existence. I was angry with anyone who was *not* suffering from the physical ailments I experienced, and I was angry with anyone suffering from the same ailments. The problem with anger—or perhaps, the saving grace—is that it quickly becomes senseless, and in the end all I knew was that I should be angry even if I didn't know what I was angry about. It ages the body when anger festers within. Getting my emotions in order was my salvation from the toxicity of anger and bitterness.

Compassion fatigue, born of anger, soon developed into victim mentality. I could not see life beyond the bubble of pain I had created for myself. As I lived in that bubble, I wanted everyone who saw me to feel sorry for me, and I blamed everything on someone or something. But being a victim of my circumstances revealed a crippling fear. Afraid that things would not improve, I grew astoundingly self-critical.

I participated in ultra-marathons to prove to my body that I was not defeated. I trained hard, I worked ridiculously long hours, I went on ridiculous diets I shudder to think about even now. For two months, I drank only water and ate two eggs per day. It was terrible. I was sabotaging my body so that the ailments wouldn't have a body to plague.

Ironically, I have autoimmune disease. My body destroys itself, and I was deliberately assisting the destruction of my body to *fix* the ailments.

Living life from a defeated viewpoint was another major obstacle I had to learn to overcome. I had to learn to love myself, to be kind to my body. And most importantly, I had to forgive myself for all the hurt I was imposing on myself. It was a grueling but necessary process. Every day is a chance to heal and find the balance and self-acceptance necessary for growth.

Defining Moments

Defining moments are more of a process than the singular occurrences the phrase suggests. For me, the defining moments have been a journey that is nothing short of miraculous. In 2015 I was a Businesswoman of the Year finalist, and this recognition boosted my battered esteem and gave me reason to smile, get up, and show up.

Two amazing people in my life, Marvin and Zinzi, encouraged me to write a book because I had a story to tell, and it did wonders for my healing.

It encouraged me to write a piece for *Nguvu*, a collaboration for women of African descent. When it received positive reviews, the author in me was born. I have been writing ever since. Writing my first book, *Pain, Heartache &*

Forgiveness was a breeze because, by then, I knew the author had been in me all along.

I also found my voice in other ways, in speaking for the purpose of helping others heal. But before doing that, I had to go for therapy to find my own healing. Divorce gave me a second chance at life and relationships, I am deeply grateful that I got to start again. In 2018 I moved from Namibia to Zimbabwe and I got appointed the country head for *First Class On Your Becoming*, the sisterhood of women becoming together. In 2019 I was called back to Namibia to be honored as Woman of the Year in recognition of the work I had been doing for women, cancer patients, and survivors for more than ten years. And I was selected as a Tony Elumelu Foundation entrepreneur.

I was also blessed with an amazing sisterhood of supportive, empathic, understanding women who have played an amazing role in my healing, growth, transformation. I would not have become who I am today without my tribe of sisters.

Life before success

There was a time I wallowed in immense self-doubting. For reasons I've already described, my self-esteem had suffered a huge blow. I discovered that my husband had cheated on me. He *told* me to my face that he was cheating on me because I was not *needing* him enough, and that my sickness was raining on his parade. I went through a humiliating phase of seeking validation from others. Even as I spoke at conferences, I was affected by self-doubt.

During one such conference, midway through a speech, the self-doubt kicked in, and for a whole minute I forgot what I was speaking on. I recall reflecting on what I was even doing in front of all those people, as if I was even worthy enough to be a presenter. Miraculously, my speech came back to me and I finished without incident.

But the worst was not over. After delivering my speech, I walked around asking people how I did. I was so in need of validation, I asked if they found my speech inspiring before they had a chance to criticize it.

One other very unattractive behavior that I also adopted during my rock-bottom phase was being an apologist. Apologizing became my way of life. Anything that made me stand out or appear different from those around me triggered a chain of apologies. It was tiring and taxing and a perpetual burden.

Wallowing in self-pity is not sexy on anyone, but I found myself rocking self-pity like a "boss." The problem with throwing myself pity parties was that I became very selfish, wanting everyone to join in and have their lives revolve around me. If any conversation was not about me and what was happening in my life, I didn't want any part of it.

It's tiring and emotionally draining to not care about others and to make it all about yourself. It made me forget how to be happy; to smile. I remember telling a friend that I was afraid I would never be happy again because I was too broken to mend or fix. I am glad I can now talk about that part of my life in the past tense.

My maiden surname is Kamba, which means *tortoise*. And true to my kambaness, I retreated into my shell and shut out anyone and everyone who dared come close. It was a confusing state to be in because I wanted everyone to feel my pain but, at the same time, I didn't want anyone in my space. I had so much anger in my heart.

Writing was my saving grace. Acknowledging that my writings were going to be seen by the public made me realize that staying in my shell was only a cry for attention. Through my writing, I was saying *Look at me*. But in other ways, I was shouting *Don't look at me*. And even if you do look at me, you won't find me, because I'm in my shell.

Success look

This beautiful journey of becoming the best version of myself has led me to my golden thread. It's the WHY to my doing what I do, to my living the way I live and, above all, to my being who I am in all my actions and choices, believing in my purpose and accepting that I am a conduit for the healing of others. In a world that is so hung up on chasing after money, I have become aware that wealth is not defined by money, but by the many blessings you have in life.

Appreciating that I do not know everything has made me seek mentorship from others. I am fortunate enough to be a Cherie Blair Foundation for Women mentee with a wonderful mentor who has opened my eyes to so many possibilities for continued success and growth. I can summarize my success as wholeheartedly loving what I do and who I am becoming, being at peace with myself and everyone around me, and with attempting to light the way for others to find their own healing in order to become their best.

Advice on personal growth

Breathe.

Breathe through the pain. Remember all the times you have been in pain and have come out strong.

Becoming is a metamorphosis that hurts, stretches and pulls.

Breathe and trust that you can survive this, too.

Becoming is a process of faith and hope.

Breathe and believe that this is part of the process.

Becoming is never a destination.

Breathe your way into your Becoming.

What I stand for

I once had an epiphany that all I need and must be is Love, Peace, and Light—to myself and to the world around me. These three elements have since become me and what I stand for.

My mission is to inspire my soul sisters to rise above their circumstances and to dare to be bold.

Soul success

I define Soul Success as holistic success, which is the epitome of becoming the very best of ourselves. When we have attained it, we become emotionally, physically, mentally, spiritually, and financially fulfilled and balanced.

Emotional success means being brave enough to scrape off the scab covering the festering emotional wounds that I had so skillfully covered up and hid from the world, allowing myself to be vulnerable and raw. With self-love, support from my tribe of sisters, and seeking help from a therapist, I finally managed to find healing and self-acceptance. I can now share my story unapologetically and, most importantly, help fellow sisters find the same emotional healing. As I grow, I achieve this emotional success every day, and I have learned to celebrate each day positively. Happiness is a choice I make.

Physical success, for me, has been learning to accept that it's okay to be different and to appreciate that I am not in competition with anyone. After fourteen surgical operations, I am allowed to feel the way I feel and am not obliged to explain myself. I am kinder to myself. I exercise to stay fit. I nourish my body. I take the necessary supplements. And, above all, I rest. I have a new and beautiful relationship with my body. It communicates to me, and I not only listen but I am also compassionate with myself. For the first time in my life I am living in harmony with my body, and I am happier, more content, and more comfortable in my own melanin-popping skin.

Mental success has been finding the inner strength to not give a fuck about what the naysayers, the haters, and the negative people say about me. I stay centered by doing yoga and meditating, which translates to positive cognitions—choosing to allow the inspiring, transformational, positive, nurturing, and fun stuff to occupy my mind. Every day, I make the conscious choice to be love, peace, and light to everyone, everywhere.

Spiritual success, or awakening, has gently guided me into the realization that without choosing to love unconditionally, to be at peace, and to shine my light, I cannot enjoy spiritual success. Becoming these three essential traits has afforded me liberty, contentment, and inner joy. Every day I purpose to become better than the previous day in this journey I have chosen to embark on.

Financial success is one journey that I would have not fully comprehended had I not learned that it is not the ultimate goal. It is merely a reward by the universe for the servitude and desire to impact other lives to find healing and purpose. I have come to understand that money is an energy, and when I am harmoniously aligned with myself, my environment, and the universe, it naturally flows to me.

Barbara's 5 Steps to Soul Success

1. Stop making excuses. Fear is the number one source for excuses, so it is important to acknowledge our fears, seek help to look fear in the face, and be willing to take the first step toward becoming who we want to be and who we are meant to be.

2. Drop everything that is toxic. These can be behaviors, choices, friends, relationships, habits, thoughts, and environments. Allowing yourself to be this raw and vulnerable has tremendous rewards.

3. Run/Walk toward life, healing, freedom, grace, growth and transformation.

4. Rest/Take a break from all cares and allow yourself to replenish and rejuvenate.

5. Forgive yourself and others; don't fall victim to anger and bitterness.

PILLAR 3

Money

"Formal education will make you a living. Self-education will make you a fortune."
— Jim Rohn

Money used to feel like a nasty curse word. If you cared about it, you were evil. Growing up, my family and I lived a modest, simple life. We were all happy and we didn't need money to make us happy. My parents got married at 18 and had my oldest sister at 19. They raised my two older sisters off of a college budget. My father eventually became a journalist and sportswriter, while my mother manages dental offices. They landed good jobs and made a good life for all of us.

We lived modestly and were happy. Growing up with this mentality, I had subconsciously made up the lie that rich people were evil because they sought happiness in all the wrong places. Because money to me was evil, I decided that I would ignore it. In my early twenties, I got my first credit card. I had no idea what to do with that until I maxed it out and pretended the bill didn't exist. Money never made sense to me. You could tell me that I'd owe you $100 or $100,000 and it would feel the same to me.

I didn't understand how to nurture and develop a relationship with money until it slapped me right in the face and I was broke, homeless, and was $100,000 deep in student loans. Now don't feel too sorry for me because when I say I was homeless, I wouldn't ever attempt to say that I know what it's like to be living on the streets and hungry for food. I still had places to go; I surfed on friends' couches until I was forced to move back in with the parents. At the same time, I was completely lost and hungry to gain my power and independence.

My relationship with money was toxic until I surrounded myself with mentors who would teach me how to respect, nurture, and love it. It wasn't an easy path, though. In my first business I was making six figures, but at the end of month I was still stressed out about bills. On the surface I seemed well off to others, but deep down I was always suffering financially.

We need to do better in this realm, and that starts with women gaining the tools to be financial powerhouses. We need to feel good about making money instead of apologizing when we request it. In my experience working with clients, most women are undercharging. We feel bad when someone says, "I can't afford it," and because we care so much, we end up helping them for free, anyway. Now don't get me wrong, sister. There's a time and a place for community service and contribution. But if you're always giving yourself away for free, you'll never be able to impact people the way you want. This is why money is an important and necessary pillar to Soul Success. Like any relationship we'd have with a lover, we must gain the tools to nurture our relationship with money. Abundance is all around us, but only when we choose it.

On my quest for financial success, I had always secretly hoped my prince would save me from my self-inflicted struggles. I would find a nice man with an honest job who could help me get out of debt. That's the problem with old Disney Princess movies: They tell us that our prince can save us instead of giving us the tools to save ourselves. Those movies have changed since then. I love the story of Moana who independently saves the heart of Te Fiti to save her island. No prince involved. I love watching the sisterly bond between Ana and Elsa and the magic they channel to save Arendelle from destruction. The shakti rising. Times are changing with these stories and I'm grateful that my daughters will grow up with the message that we are the creators of our own destiny. We can be whoever we want to be.

At the same time, we still have work to do. Women are still making only 80 cents for every dollar a man makes. We are behind the curve. Although 46% of financial services employees are women, only 15% of women are at the executive level. Men still dominate this sector. This is why money is a necessary pillar to Soul Success. Women can be financial powerhouses. You can be a financial powerhouse!

CHAPTER 11

F*%*& to Financial Freedom

S ara and I met inside a mastermind group. I'd show up on our regularly scheduled Zoom calls and Sara would always pop on a minute early with a bright shining smile. From the moment I first met her at our Zoom meeting, I knew she was a big deal. Her energy is contagious, and every time we connected was another opportunity to get excited about life.

I found out from another gal in our group that she had been featured on Oprah. Mother freakin' Oprah Winfrey! I have to say freakin' because if I use Oprah and the f-word in the same sentence, I'm fairly certain I'll go to hell. Sara is not one to toot her own horn, so I know about all her accomplishments via other people, along with a little bit of online research.

Sara has also been featured on NPR, Good Morning America, Katie Couric, Fox, The View. She is a bestselling author coach, teaches at Northwestern, and is the creator of *Thought Leader Academy.* She is a real, life-breathing unicorn.

One day on our mastermind call, I expressed my deep desire to publish a book of memoirs. I told the group how empty I felt inside because this idea had been brewing inside of me for a while. My dream of publishing a series of books had been sitting for years, but I had at least one million legitimate reasons why I should wait. I was frustrated.

The minute we got off our call, Sara sent me a voice memo: "Megan, there's something about you and your book concept that's calling me toward you. Your ideas are brilliant and I feel strongly that your book has the ability to impact many people. No pressure if you're feeling resistance, but I completely feel you're on to something."

It was something about her belief in me and the book that sparked the fire I had been burying for so long. Less than a month later and this entire book was sent to the editor. Sara helped me manage the project, writing a 200+ page book in a matter of weeks. She is the reason this magical gift is in your hands right now. I can honestly say that I couldn't have done it without her. I thank God I made the decision to smell her unicorn farts. Now I'm starting to feel like a unicorn myself, and that's something to celebrate!

Sara Connell

> "No one is afraid for you if you're going to be a
> chemical engineer, yet people worry greatly if you
> say you are going to be an artist"
> — Elizabeth Gilbert TED 2009

Sunlight streamed through the stained-glass window in our kitchen as I made my declaration to my mother.

"I want to be a writer."

My Great Grandmother had passed a few years before we acquired the dome glass window with its crescent shapes of jewel reds, yellows, blues and lead borders. I was fifteen and, as my mother balanced her checkbook with the blue plastic cover folded open on the white table, pen scratching paper, the window gave the room the feeling of church.

"I want to be a writer," I said again.

I'd likely made this declaration before. I'd been filling journals and notebooks, reading five library books a week for years. This time, I was fifteen, about to enter high school. The intention felt real.

My mother put her *Bic* pen on the table and sighed.

"I don't think that would be good for you," she said. "You're not good with money. And you like nice things."

I didn't understand what her first point had to do with being a writer, but I sensed a lack of enthusiasm. My mother was not trying to be a dream crusher. She would have piped up that I had other strengths. If you wanted someone to recite eight Shakespeare sonnets by memory, I was your woman. Create an original play with no budget and kids in the neighborhood as actors to raise money for special education at the school? Done. It was the 90's, so my mother did not say, "Go to college and meet a nice, rich man, and pump out some kids for him." In fact, even having married my father in the 70's, my mother was the economic engine of our family. She'd graduated with honors as an Economics major at Trinity University and was accepted into Wharton (she didn't go—married my father instead—but she *was* accepted). She pays the bills, keeps the household budget in her head, and after my youngest sister went to kindergarten, she started a career that in the end would out-earn my father's.

My mother advised me against a writing career out of fear. Fear that I'd end up sleeping on the couch in the basement at thirty years of age, as so many catastrophizing articles about my generation predict. Fear that I'd struggle worse than we struggle as a family financially. If college graduates with degrees in computer science and engineering end up failing to launch, what kind of financial chance would an artist have? The world has offered the model to its citizens for centuries—as it has to all of us. Artists shivering in garrets, dying of syphilis in the streets, selling their hair or forgoing food to buy canvases and paint.

I wonder, too, how much Catholicism factored in her response. Modesty, humility, service were the important values. I was supposed to work a respectable, stable job and be neither wealthy nor destitute. And gender must have compounded her fears. Women already earned less than twenty-five percent than their male counterparts. Financially, the odds were against me.

The idea that I could be a successful writer, not living in my mother's basement at 30, didn't factor into her equation. The message to me was clear: I didn't have what it took to be successful with money.

I spend the next two decades proving her right.

I went on to become a published writer, but I did struggle financially. I'm "not good with money" with prowess. It would be years before I confronted my patterns of scarcity, lack, money obsession, worry, low financial self-esteem. It would be more than ten years into my adult life before I started to unravel those threads. The journey led me to a Money Workshop.

Since sharing someone else's spiritual experience at a workshop is about as exciting as sharing someone's most recent dental cleaning, I'll spare the details and get right to the question that changed everything: The workshop leader, a spirited young man who made his first million at twenty-five, asked, "What is your earliest memory of money?"

First, a few experiences and memories that did not occur to me: Seeing my mother balance the checkbook at that kitchen table every Saturday; the burn of shame felt when a parent at the Catholic school I attended asked if I needed her daughter's old uniform or school shoes.

We never went hungry, and my parents paid their mortgage on time, or early. But especially in the years before my mother went back to work, I wore hand-me-downs from my cousins and we ate food that was on sale at the grocery store. We spent summers at the neighborhood pool in the blistering sun, burning our feet on the concrete terrace, where lifeguards provided free babysitting. My sisters and I heard "We can't afford it" as often as the Madonna songs that played incessantly on the radio.

It is not lost on me that I speak from some level—however modest it may have seemed to me—of privilege. Swimming in a community pool in the summer and living with two parents in a house they owned, with more than enough food, put me in the top ten percent of kids on this planet in terms of wealth and resources. None of which was mine on the strength of personal merit, but merely by my birth as a white female in America. Even early on, I recognized this. But I heard Marianne Williamson once say, "You being broke does not serve the world."

Perhaps even more because of my privilege, I began to balk at the poverty I was creating. I understood that if I was ever going to make the impact and contribution that would actually help all people attain more, I was going to have to break my commitment to scarcity.

Back to the Money Workshop. My memory mechanism did not think of any of these early financial experiences. I didn't consider the fact that my father, who entered the seminary at nineteen and nearly became a Catholic priest, had taken a vow of poverty at nineteen. I didn't consider the role of religion or gender or artistic archetypes. Neither did I connect my lack of earning power to the memory of a friend's father reaching for me during a sleepover when I was eight and pulling me into his bed—the effect of that event on my finances would come much later.

What came instead was me at six years old, on Thanksgiving Day, when my Great Aunt Mary pressed a perfectly crisp $100 bill into my fingers.

Great Aunt Mary sent $5 bills tucked in Hallmark birthday cards every February. But that Thanksgiving, my hands shook with that hundred-dollar bill in them. I'd never seen so much money in one place. Benjamin Franklin's merry face all but winked at me. I hugged Aunt Mary and put the bill into my pocket. I walked to the living room, unpocketed the bill, and proudly showed the gift to my father.

"It's too much," he said, and he took Ben from my hands. He clenched his jaw, and I cried as he slid the bill back into Aunt Mary's brown handbag that sat on the top step.

After we uncovered our first financial memories, the Money Workshop facilitator asked a follow-up question:

"What story did you make up about yourself and money from this experience?"

I didn't deserve it, I wrote. I am not allowed to have a lot of money.

These were my money beliefs as I entered the world after college:

I'm not good with money

I don't deserve money

The vow of poverty was passed down to me

Writers can't make money

I'm not allowed to have money

I was twenty-four and I still didn't think I could *make it*. My family was concerned for my future, but there was nothing I wanted to do but write—so I put my attention into pursuing my dream of becoming a published author.

The writing dream is not easy to fulfill. I have nearly as many doubts about my ability to get my writing published as I do about ever earning a cent doing so.

I met the man who would become my husband at an advertising job I took to pay my bills. Amazingly, we had the chance to move to England—a mutual dream of ours—for his work. We got engaged, shoved our paltry possessions into storage, and boarded the next British Airways flight to London.

In London, I walked the very streets where many of my literary heroes penned the books that would define their lives and live on long after they left their physical form. I fell down a delicious rabbit hole of life coaching, holistic medicine, and shamanism, and because I couldn't get a work visa without a marriage certificate, I wrote every day. I walked through Hyde Park and over the Thames Bridges, wandered through the British museum war rooms, spent an entire day with Frieda Khalo's unabridged paintings at the *Tate Modern*. In a few months, I cranked out a three-hundred-page novel. I was happy. Bill and I got married. I was finally a writer.

Rent in London is three times as much as it was in Chicago where we'd met. Six months into our marriage, we were burning through Bill's paychecks like matchsticks.

"You have to get a job," he said.

I burned, too, as I realized I had become a dependent, not a partner, of Bill's. I had brought in zero dollars, zero pounds as a writer. If we were going to continue to live abroad, we needed a second income.

I contemplated my options. I'd written a novel but was petrified to show my work to anyone. I had no idea how to get published or earn money writing. So I looked to my burgeoning other love—holistic medicine and personal growth. I found a job managing a homeopathic clinic on The Kings Road in Chelsea where I earned exactly the amount, down to the pound, that Bill and I needed to cover the gap in paying our bills.

I don't deserve money.

We cut back on a few things and I saved enough to invest in training and licensing as a holistic therapist and life coach. This would be the work to support me while I wrote at night.

Writers can't make money.

When Bill's assignment in London ended, we moved back to Chicago, and I started my coaching practice. I did powerful work with clients and I made a little bit of money: $20,000 one year, $15,000 another—so minimal that our accountant told me several years in a row I would likely not have to pay federal taxes. I abandoned the book I wrote in England. I studied craft. I wrote a new manuscript and beseeched the Universe to help me publish the work. Everything I watched and read declared that you need to be published to get published. You need connections with agents, or you need to be a celebrity. I was utterly unconnected. Finally, I met someone who knew a literary agent.

"She won't for sure take you on or anything," he said, "but she'll probably take a phone call. I've got one ask with her: Are you sure what you have is good enough?"

Please…Of course I wasn't sure. I believed I had potential as a writer about one out of every one hundred days. I sent my manuscript to the agent, anyway. On the appointed day, with shaking fingers, I dialed her number in New York.

"If you're willing to do some significant revisions," she said, "I'll consider representing you."

It wasn't the "Wow! You're brilliant, this is the next bestseller!" that I had hoped for, but I had a chance!

You might imagine I would run to my laptop, type feverishly with every shred of energy in my body until the revisions were complete—but I didn't. I sat in cold sweats, my laptop dark as a grave. The dread I felt was so intense my eyes watered. What if I tried my absolute hardest and failed? What if she confirmed what I'd feared all those years? That I was simply not good enough.

A day went by. A week. Two weeks. At the end of week three, I saw my dream hanging in the air in front of me like a mirage. I was going to sink before I left the harbor.

All that time, I had been coaching women on changing careers, pursuing their art, and recovering, as I was, from trauma. One of my clients mentioned a Writing Coach in Northern California. I'm a coach myself, yet I resisted hiring a coach. I didn't want to invest the money, didn't want to admit my weakness and cowardice. I wanted to figure this out on my own.

But desperation moved me, and I made the call. That coach helped me through the revisions. In June, I flew to New York and presented the revised manuscript to the agent, and she signed me. I was a writer with an agent. The dream was happening.

That moment in Grammercy Tavern, facing the Flatiron building, led to a book deal, appearing on Oprah and being published in *The New York Times*. If I had ever doubted the coaching profession, I didn't then. I threw myself deeper into the craft of writing and my coaching with the dedication of a zealot.

***

Two years later, Bill and I were in our accountant's office to pay our taxes.

"You need to make more money."

I felt the slick of déjà vu all over me, as if we'd never left London, and I was making no money. My first book sold well, but I'd been given a large advance, all of which I had spent on book promotion and the nanny who came to the house to take care of my son three days a week while I wrote the book. The advance had just earned out, so we weren't receiving much in royalties. We'd already wiped out our savings in the eight rounds of IVF fertility treatments we'd undergone to have our miraculous baby, and I was still making somewhere between $30,000 a year coaching.

You're not good with money.

Writers can't make money.

Coaches apparently didn't make much either. The depressing statistic that most coaches earn less than $25,000 a year had come across my Facebook feed more than once.

Shame and fear wrapped me like a snake. I was doing good work—I could feel it. I saw the results. My clients started businesses and found partners. They healed illnesses, they got married and found creative success. But something needed to change. I was a crustacean stuffed into a too-small shell. I wanted desperately to crack this cycle of lack and under-earning, but I didn't know how. My husband and son deserved better from me. And I wanted more for myself.

Around then, I drove to Milwaukee to teach a coaching workshop. In the car, a podcast guest told the host about a study that demonstrated "Your life and income will reflect the five people with whom you spend the most time."

I thought about my friends and colleagues. Lots of artists and coaches—passionate, generous, talented individuals doing amazing work in the world and none earning what they want to earn. Most are not comfortably supporting themselves. Not a single one has what I'd call financial abundance.

I pulled the car to the shoulder. Did this mean I needed to vacate all of my current relationships? The next week I heard a coach online say, "You can only take your clients as far as you have gone." In many areas of my coaching—creativity, spirituality, personal growth—I could take someone quite far. Financially, though? Did my clients and my family deserve a coach who was just one more example of the under-earning, if not starving artist and coach?

I got home from Milwaukee and did what I do when I need wisdom: I go to the trees. For three months, I walked in every woods, park, and nature preserve I could drive to in

Illinois and Wisconsin. And I emerged from this time with two clear directives:

1. What I loved, I realized, was helping people with the calling to write and to make a positive impact on the world—to become successful, published authors and speakers. I needed to give up general coaching and specialize.

2. I needed to get *into the room* with people three, five, twenty steps ahead of me financially. I needed to immerse myself with writers and coaches making the kind of money I wanted to make—and in a way that I admired: six figures, seven figures, or more per year.

That summer I burned the boats. I closed the coaching practice I had been running and birthed a new business: helping writers and thought leaders change the world with their stories. I researched high-end coaching programs and invested $10,000 in a business coaching program with people in my industry making six figures a year. I had $10,001 in my bank account the day I made the payment. I vomited as the card was charged and the payment notification came through. With no precedent, I trusted myself (*I'm not good with money*). I declared I would make the investment back in three months. Eleven weeks later, I had made $10,300—more than I typically made in six months. I started publishing short writing pieces in magazines. I applied for and was accepted to the Masters in Fine Arts program at Northwestern University—a degree that would allow me to make a quantum leap in my teaching, editing, and writing craft, to help my clients write award-winning books and achieve greater success.

I was saved again by coaching. In that business coaching program, I again confronted every one of those early childhood beliefs. I watched what the coaches seven steps ahead of me did and took action as if I were one of them. I did what they did even though I was terrified I would fail, that none of their strategies and structures would work for me. Through rigorous action, I cut off a thick layer of excuses, my terror of visibility, the family vow of poverty. By the end of the next year, I made $70,000. The next year I made $140,000. The third year, I brought in close to $400,000 in new business.

You can only take your clients as far as you have gone

My clients who used to make $20,000, $40,000 a year are escalating that into six figures and beyond. They became bestsellers. They give TEDx talks. Over half that annual income goes to paying talented editors, virtual assistants and team members who help propel our client's success. Last year, I founded Thought Leader Academy so that not only individuals with a calling to impact the world massively would be able to do so through books, but also through speaking and podcasts. I started hosting monthly Abundance Club meetings, a space for artists and entrepreneurs to excavate their own scarcity, lack, limiting, and those cultural and personal beliefs that were holding them back—to dissolve them and cast a new future of financial success.

I devoted myself to a new generation of the Prosperous Artist, the Rich Writer, the Eight-Figure Mission-Driven Entrepreneur. To achieve this, I kept doing the work. At every income jump, the tentacles of those old beliefs stung and sucked at me. I booked a big talk, launched a new program, broke a monthly income record, and suddenly, my amygdala was firing flares and I was sweating through my shirt.

I learned that *You don't deserve it, you can't make it, writers/coaches can't make money, and you wouldn't be good with it if you were good,* were easy to believe in. Like a greatest-hits album, the songs played over and seduced me into compliance.

Early in 2020, a client of mine, the amazing Carla Biesinger, told me that female entrepreneurs made thirty-five percent less than male entrepreneurs with the same education and in the same field. I looked it up. It was true. I believe it stems from what *The Atlantic* calls "The Confidence Gap." Women under-value and under-estimate their worth, power, and value by 25-35%. Even outside patriarchal corporate structures, women price themselves less than their male counterparts. Like the starving artist, the collective idea that women must earn less, struggle harder, deserve crumbs, etc., is etched into our feminine psyche.

And like micro concussions that eventually result in serious brain damage, trauma compounds this. There are studies that show girls who are sexually abused have a 99% chance of developing eating disorders, as well as fibromyalgia, promiscuity, sexual anorexia, addictions to alcohol and drugs. It's a crap ride that I wouldn't wish on anyone.

As I continued my work and recalled my own experiences, I wondered about the statistics of sexual abuse and financial earning. The night I was taken into that adult's bed at eight years of age left imprints on me that I may never fully comprehend and gave way to new attacks and harassment that followed me from high school to college and into the corporate world. I came away from that night in third grade believing I was broken, dirty, worthless. I would not be surprised if children who experienced sexual abuse typically earn far less than those who have not experienced such violation.

The good news: Whatever we've picked up along our unique paths—from family, society, culture, gender, from trauma or past experiences—no longer has to oppress or limit us. We're embedded with this amazing gift of brain plasticity. Every belief is revisable. Whether we want to write a book, bring a crowd of a thousand to their feet, earn a million dollars a year or create a foundation that finds ways to reverse climate change, the process is the same. Identify the lie. Revise the belief. Surround ourselves with people who've done it and are at least five steps in front of us. Do what they do. Act as if we're one of them already. Because you are.

I love *Harry Potter* and now think of personal growth as a kind of magic and this book is about turning S--- into gold. So I offer here a kind of brain alchemy—a Prosperity Potion:

I. Inventory your earliest memories/experiences/ conditioning with money. Write out every belief you inherited or took on that keeps you in the binds of lack and unworthiness. Know that it's all bulls---. You are unlimited and inherently worthy of all the Abundance of the Universe. Share the list with a trusted friend or coach. Then burn it.

II. Take a Vow of Abundance. Write your new beliefs— the ones you want to be true for you moving forward—in the form of a contract between you and The Universe. State this in the present-tense daily (e.g., I am so grateful and happy that I now know I am capable, worthy, prosperous and successful! I am one with all the abundance of the universe!

I receive more abundance every day. The more abundance I receive, the more the world wins! I receive unlimited abundance!

III. Get In the room/course/group/class/community with people making the kind of income you want to make in a way that inspires and aligns with you. This won't work if we value integrity and we go to a bunch of sales conferences with arm twisters or hard sellers. Look for, connect with, get coached by, read about, and hang out with people who hold and express your deepest values *and* are wildly prosperous in your field and other fields.

IV. Consider: My Self-Worth is my Net Worth. Shower yourself with self-care. Indulge in pleasure. Give yourself breaks. Know that every time you disprove a scarcity lie, you help other women and all people do it, too. Know that your very thoughts have the power to create a shift in Abundance consciousness on this planet. Do it for yourself. Do it for your clients, readers, and friends. Do it for the next generation.

CHAPTER 12

Public School Teacher to 7-Figures

In the fall of 2019, I hosted an online show called the "Rock Your Money Summit." When I asked my community for top money experts, Jesse was one of the first to be recommended. I met her a few times online to see if she was going to be a fit and I immediately knew the answer was a *Hell Yes.*

Jesse and I became fast friends and would schedule zoom *coffee dates* just to stay connected and catch up on what we were working on. We share the same values in spirituality and business. After hanging up, I would leave our conversations feeling so refreshed that there was another person also advocating financial prosperity for healers and spiritual entrepreneurs. Too many healers are suffering financially and, quite frankly, I'm sick of it. It didn't take long for me to realize that I needed to have her speak on stage at my events and feature her in this book.

Jesse went from public high school teacher to seven-figure business in just two years. How was it that someone like Jesse could experience such radical transformation in such a short period of time? This is why I had to have her here with you right now; to give you practical tools you can begin implementing to find financial abundance in your life.

Jesse Johnson

You know those spiritual teachers and healers who are constantly manifesting, working with the law of attraction, but generally also struggling to pay the rent, right? Well those are my people—I help them build seven-figure businesses and thrive in full alignment with their purpose.

We are at a tipping point: human consciousness is evolving, and evolving fast. In order to manage, negotiate, and navigate those changes, the world needs guides, healers, support. If those healers and guides and coaches don't understand money, they can't help the world *integrate* that healing into material experience. Money must be included.

In my experience, not only is this integration necessary for the growth of the world, it's powerful for us as spiritual practitioners, too. My own spiritual practice has been exponentially elevated by having a business, mastering sales, and integrating money as a consciousness practice. It has demanded that I *live* my practice, not only on the cushion or the mat, but in every moment, every breath, every interaction.

My mission is to help the world's guides, healers, and mentors integrate their spiritual mastery with money, and to understand that making money is the most spiritual thing they can do.

I didn't always know this.

I was raised by two therapists—loving, middle-class parents who worked hard, believed in the value of discipline, and held an incredibly high standard for connection and emotional fluency. I learned very early on that connection, talking about feelings, and self-awareness were critically important, and I am grateful to still carry that understanding today. Connection, intimacy, and love matter to me first and foremost.

Despite growing up in a relatively segregated small town in North Carolina, I missed the memo on contemporary racism and injustice. My high school studies of the civil rights movement had me thinking we were done with that part of history. It wasn't until I got to college that I realized how much injustice was still at work in the world. Clarity struck. I deeply cared about being of service, giving back, and helping people. And I didn't really want to make too much money—I already had so much privilege. Who was I to have more money?

So I did the natural, logical thing: I started teaching high school math in New York City public schools.

I loved the work. I got to express and experience deep connections, build life-changing relationships with my students and my colleagues every day. We were working on really interesting, complex problems together, and it created bonds that nourished my soul. And I *knew* I was being of service; every single moment of my life as a teacher was designed to help my kids, to share my wealth, to give back.

I taught in my own classroom for seven years, and then transitioned to coaching math teachers and principals in public schools all over New York City for another five years. At the end of my career in math education, I was working with 82 schools across the Bronx, Brooklyn, Manhattan. After those twelve years of passion and mission-driven work to dismantle the cycle of poverty, I hit a wall.

I had become a masterful educator and coach, yet despite my deep connections with my students and colleagues, despite my deep commitment to service, I wasn't seeing lasting impact at the systemic level. Public schools are still rooted in scarcity. There aren't enough teachers, time, or textbooks. There isn't enough money. There isn't enough love. Sometimes, there aren't even enough desks.

So no matter what we were doing, no matter how deeply the connection and the service was present, the impact just wasn't sticking. And the frustration of beating my head against that particular wall was making me miserable. I was angry at colleagues, ready to quit fighting the system that I felt was fighting me.

I wanted more.

I wanted connection, service, *and* impact.

I just didn't know how to make it happen.

The realization that I wanted more put me onto a new path: looking for the new career and lifestyle that would allow me to live into these deep desires. It took me about a year to figure out what was next for me as I searched high and low for what possible future there was to leverage all of my skills and enthusiasm.

Three minutes in one conversation turned that tide: I spoke to the woman I would hire as my first coach. I listened to her articulate that all the things I wanted, plus freedom and money, were all possible *in my own business.*

This had been a blind spot for me. I didn't think of myself as entrepreneurial, and I didn't even sell Girl Scout cookies growing up. I thought I knew nothing about the world of business and sales.

Who knew?

In two years, I went from startup to seven figures. Two years. I had no idea that was possible.

Let's talk about the money. How did I do it?

I've already told you about three things I did leading up to this point, and they're worth repeating.

1. KNOW YOUR GIFT. I knew I had a gift that wanted to express itself more fully in the world. My confidence and fuel supply originate here—not in messaging or branding, but in that full-bodied soul knowing.

2. WANT MORE. This was not a trivial kind of wanting more. I had trained myself, like man us, tolerate less, want less, ask for less. And it was only because of the *contrast* of my day-to-day experience that I broke that pattern and chose to reach for more.

3. HIRE A MENTOR. It was my first coach who helped me understand that what I wanted was a business, and I hired her to help me build it. I didn't have to reinvent the wheel. She called me on my shit. She showed me what was possible, and both inspired and demanded more greatness from me.

I now know how essential these first three steps are. They build a strong foundation on which any big vision can be created.

From there, I went through three more significant steps to build my business and create a lifestyle, home, relationship, and spiritual practice that I love.

My fourth step was to make the decision to change. To put my stake in the ground, commit to my vision, and get my ass on the line. I sort of did this when I hired my mentor, but the bigger decision came when I needed to quit my school job, change my email signature, and put myself out there as a life coach.

The decision felt like skydiving.

You're up in the airplane dangling your little legs off that ledge, looking 10,000 feet below. It's not too late to back out. Your butt is still on the floor, you can still feel gravity resting you on some semblance of earth. You've still got to make that damn decision—otherwise, they're just going to fly you back down to earth. You can claim your gift, want more, hire coaches forever, and still not change.

And growth around money is particularly uncomfortable for many of us; we've all got an edge around money. Making the decision to change your income, your class, how you make and spend money isn't difficult, but it is massively uncomfortable and very few people do it. Similar to jumping out of an airplane, we are biologically designed *not* to do it. Our brains have not had the millions of years that they need to catch up to our physical reality, which tells us we *can* be safe jumping out of an airplane. Our brains are programmed, by no fault of anyone, to prevent us from doing this. Changing your class is the same. It was absolutely terrifying. And I did it. I made the decision to change.

And when I did, everything else changed, too. The people I wanted to spend time with shifted. The way I saw the world changed. My taxes increased, along with my income, and my spending.

When you make that two-millimeter pivot to fall out of the plane, your sense of earth is gone. All sense of the familiar is gone.

And when you make the decision to change, that's when you call in the resources you wouldn't otherwise know you had: namely, the resilience to freefall, and to enjoy the thrill of it. The freedom to feel the air as you fall and enjoy the support of the parachute when it's time for landing.

I jumped out of the airplane before understanding my business; that came later. I'd call it my fifth step. The *How* of my business was not difficult, and I find this kind of strategy fun and creative. Crafting a vision of who I really wanted to work with, how I could help them, what I wanted the final result of our impactful work to be, and how I wanted it to feel while we were doing it—this is the fun part: the freefall, the vision from the air, the fast ride.

After landing on the earth with all that clarity, the next step was sales. It was time to get my work out into the world, shine my light, and actually do the thing. Building a business demands that our material around money be addressed head on. No one else can make the money for you. You've got to do it. And this realization showed me the limit of my faith. It showed me where I didn't actually believe in myself, where I didn't believe in God. Money demanded that I shine a light on the limitations I was still putting on myself, on others, and on God.

Sales mastery challenged me in every possible way. I was afraid of rejection, trained to avoid the no. I was deeply co-dependent, waiting with bated breath for someone, anyone, to say yes and affirm that this whole business was a good idea.

Cold calls were brutal for me, and I made hundreds of them. Cold calls taught me to fall in love with sales, get deeply curious about people, and stay present no matter what was coming at me.

I like to say now that everything people like about me comes from my sales mastery. Sales showed me all the things that were out of integrity, unconscious, and downright manipulative in me, and demanded that I clear that shit out. FAST!

It is because of sales that I found my true authority, mastered my form of channeling, learned the truth of service, and how often it needs to come out by speaking an uncomfortable truth.

My coach helped me set my first financial goal. When I met that goal the first time, it completely transformed what I knew to be possible. It was the first time I saw my subconscious programming dissolve. It was then that I began to understand how to approach the issue of *changing class*, something that I never was able to teach my students. I had no idea how to teach my low-income kids how to become middle class or more. I didn't even know how *I* had become middle-class!

I couldn't provide them with that service *then*. Now, I can. With my coaching clients, I've witnessed that this process works—not just for me, but for anyone who is ready and willing to do the work.

Here's one true story—and there are many—to demonstrate how quickly it can happen.

One of my favorite clients had been masterful as a healer, psychic, and transformational coach; in business for 10 years; very confident about her skillset; very confident about the results that she got for her clients. But she was struggling to pay her rent month after month. Money was coming in, and that same money was going out even faster.

And for fun, I'll share with you that this client didn't go on Google to find me. She went to God. She meditated. She looked inward. She listened to her inner guidance. And she asked, "What am I missing? What am I not seeing that has me struggling so much? I teach people to be free, not to struggle, so why am I struggling?"

That same day, she met me at an event and recognized the answer to her inner question. She thought, "Maybe this is the answer." She did a little internet stalking, watched my YouTube videos, and knew that there was something for us to do together.

She called me in tears, "Jesse, because of you I've realized I want a seven-figure business. I have no idea how to do that. I don't even know how to consistently bring in the money that I need right now. But I know I'm here for great things, and I want to break through."

I said, "Girl, I got you. I know exactly what you need to do because I've done it. I see you. I know what you're capable of." She hired me on the spot. In six weeks, she had added a zero to her monthly income, going from $2,000 to $20,000 almost immediately. That's how fast this change happens.

Her example reinforces this truth that the work around money does not have to be hard.

It's not hard to make money. In fact, it's easier to make more money than less. We work hard to not make money!

In addition to reaching her money goals, this client met an amazing man during our work together. She learned how to receive. She opened up those channels to receive not only money and support, but also love—more connection in her divine collaboration. That's another part of the power of opening to money. It's the most spiritual thing we can do.

Would you like to make seven figures in your business? Is that an authentic desire for you? It may feel a little terrifying.

But if you really want it, it *should* feel scary—it goes against your subconscious programs.

AND it should also feel really fucking exciting!

When you're bringing seven figures and more into your business:

You will be able to help more people, not less.

You will have the resources to employ more people, not less.

You will be able to actually support yourself and ensure that the impact you know you're here for, that divine purpose that's moving through you, actually comes to fruition.

Bringing in seven figures and more is widening the gate to let everything that is meant to come *to* you come, and everything that's meant to come *through* you, comes through. Both are very powerful.

The most spiritual thing you can do is make money—it is your purpose to do so. You are meant to have all that you need and more. When you're living out your highest purpose, fulfilling your unique vision of service, and you are fully supported and thriving in all areas of your life, that's what soul success looks like.

My biggest piece of advice for readers is to *take action*. It's not enough to read this book — although it's a great starting point. If you want new results, you must take new action. The awareness is essential: absolutely work with your inner material and resistance. Then *put it into practice*. Do the outer work as well. You'll find that digging into the practices of business, sales, and money mastery is the most powerful tool for transforming your consciousness.

Here's an exercise to help you make this concrete:

Write down your current average monthly income. Feel what that number feels like in your body. Where does it resonate when you think about that amount coming in again this month? How does it feel? Where do you get excited? Where do you feel the limitation of it? What do you know it's going to go to? It's one of the most common things I hear, "It just goes right back out. It comes in, right back out." Feel that, too. Feel it coming in and going out.

Now put another zero on the end of that number... And feel the difference in your body. So if you were thinking $10,000 a month, now you're thinking $100,000 a month. If you were thinking $2,000 a month, now you're thinking $20,000 a month. If you were thinking $50,000 a month, now you're thinking $500,000 a month.

How does that number feel in your body? What changes in your confidence? in your enthusiasm? in your joy? in your connection? Where do you notice discomfort around that number?

Whatever you feel about that new number shows you where your work is. How does the one who makes that money walk in the world? When she knows that all that money is coming in, how does she spend it? What does it feel like to be the one that spends that number month after month, who earns that number month after month? How would your clients be different? How would your confidence be different? How would *you* be different?

Whatever the answer is, it's time to live that way. Spend money that way. Make money that way. Make the vision real. All that you want and more is here for you. It's time for you to claim it for yourself.

Your soul's success is here.

PILLAR 4

Health

"To keep the body in good health is a duty,
otherwise we shall not be able to keep our
mind strong and clear."
— Buddha

When I first started working in the wellness industry, I became obsessed with topics like anatomy and exercise nutrition. I felt strongly that the way to change someone's life was to help them change the size of their pants. I helped my clients lose anywhere from five to a hundred pounds. I helped them train for marathons. I was obsessed, to the point where I started training for NPC Bikini Fitness Competitions to take my fitness to another level. I dropped down to 10% body fat and had abs out of nowhere. I was proud of my physique.

While I might have looked good on the outside, I didn't feel great on the inside. My soul was dying with this obsession that honestly was not healthy, despite what many trainers and magazines try to tell you.

In addition to the malnourishment, dehydration, and lack of carbohydrates, my soul was suffering. About a month before my show, my trainer didn't show up for her 6:30 am training session. It seemed to be a pattern for her. So naturally, I told the other girls that we should train each other since we showed up and she didn't. I wasn't going to waste the hour by going home.

At our next training session, she took me aside and screamed at me in front of the other girls.

"How dare you!" she said. "You're trying to steal my clients! Those are my clients, not yours. Don't try to use my successful program to benefit your business. They are onto you, you know."

I was mortified and embarrassed. What does "they are onto you" even mean? I couldn't believe she thought I was trying to steal her business. What would make her think that? Since that day, she started sharing rumors about me to the other girls in the competition. I'll spare you the petty details.

I came close to quitting at least a hundred times because I was so scared to see this woman again. She hated me. If this is what the industry was going to be like, I didn't want to have any part in it. But something inside me said that if I didn't compete, then I'd be a quitter. Even though every other part of me was telling me that I shouldn't compete, being called a quitter would mean that she had won and I had lost. Nothing seemed worse than being a quitter so, reluctantly, I competed.

When I showed up for the fitness competition, I was all alone. This trainer had a group of at least 20+ with her, some of whom were friends of mine. She told everyone in her group they couldn't talk to me, even my friend who I shared a hotel room with and referred to this trainer.

She blacklisted me.

Here I was, orange with spray tan, walking around in stripper shoes, and wearing a thong. How the hell did I get myself here? This wasn't me at all. What started as an opportunity to prove my fitness ability ended up making me feel like a freak. I hardly said a word to anyone that day, and I never even came close to winning an award.

There it was. A grown woman bullying another. How was it that I offended her so much? What did I do that triggered her? Why me? I was completely perplexed and, honestly, felt sorry for her. This woman, a powerful figure that so many other women looked up to. A woman who, during competitions looked like a 10 on the outside, was suffering so much on the inside. Only someone who is suffering can instill so much hate and judgment onto others. It reminded me of my high school experiences.

Maybe I did do something I shouldn't have? Maybe I did say something that offended her? Maybe for some reason it was *I* who was in the wrong? It will always be a mystery to me. I share this with you because my perspective on health has changed significantly since then. I realize that health is not a look, it's not a formula, and it's not just what you eat. It's not how low you can get your body fat percentage or how hot your ass looks in a thong.

It's a way of being.

That same day there was an ambulance who showed up at our competition. Apparently, this is a regular thing. Before I got on stage a male bodybuilder my age had a heart attack and passed away. We would look in the magazine and see this man as physical perfection, but this search for perfection cost him his life.

Some would have said that I looked like a strong fitness competitor. Some would have said that I was at the top of my game. But on the inside, I was suffering because I didn't have the tools to really take care of my body and my mind. Health is multidimensional, and it's not just based on body fat percentage or your metabolic index. It's how you feel. It's how you treat yourself. And maybe, it's also how you treat others.

CHAPTER 13

Endurance is the Solution

Jenn is one of my closest friends and confidants. Have you ever met a person for the first time and instantly knew you were connected on a soul level? That's Jenn to me. We've traveled together, attended conferences together, and there have been several eerie situations in which I'm fairly certain we could read each other's mind. I won't bore you with the details, but we've even encountered some crazy experiences with psychic energies, proof that our soul sisterhood runs deep.

When I first got to know Jenn, she was between businesses and went back to corporate while figuring out her next move. From what I knew at the time, she had run a successful fitness center, yoga studio, and protein bar company, not to mention was a super-hot and sexy fitness model. She invited me to lunch one day to get me up to speed on her life. Now remember, at this time I didn't know much about her at all other than what I described above. But for whatever reason, something deep within made me feel she was on the wrong path. Normally, I keep opinions like that to myself, but the nudge was strong, and for whatever reason, I was confident she would eventually receive the message from me.

"You're brilliant and you're not yet meeting your full potential," I said. "There are women who need you right now. You need to go global with your fitness business and quit your job soon."

To anyone else just meeting me, I probably would have sounded like a lunatic. Who the hell was I to tell someone I hardly knew that they needed to quit their job? This is typically not sound advice. As a business coach, I tell people they need to wait to quit their job because too many entrepreneurs end up taking this leap before they're ready financially and emotionally. There's a strategy to transition outside of the corporate world and build a sustainable business. But there was something inside me that knew I needed to deliver that news. It was her time.

A few weeks later she quit her job and hired me to help her take her business global. Yep, she's as crazy as I am. A year and a half later, she now has a wildly successful online fitness company that's highly lucrative. Not just that, but she is an in-demand speaker and influencer. Every time I talk to her, she is in a new city speaking on a different stage: IMPACT.

Jen's story is deep, profound, and not so pretty. But again, through alchemy, Jen has transformed her dark past into sparkling, shiny gold. She is the Phoenix who rose from the ashes and now she's changing thousands of lives.

Over lunch one day, Jenn looked into my eyes.

"Megan, tell me your story," she said. "What do you stand for?"

It was one of the first times I felt another soul nudging mine to play big together. I'll never forget that lunch in Phoenix. We declared our mission and shook hands in promise to one another that we would always play big together. We made a pact that we'd always have each other's backs.

Jennifer Ludington

I've been through a lot in my life. But nothing had ever hit me as hard as this.

On March 3, 2019, I received a call from my ex-husband's son while I was driving. It was a beautiful day in Sun Valley, Idaho, where I live: cold, but sunny, which is about as good as it gets in winter. I'd finished a yoga session, and I was feeling great. And I was pleasantly surprised to see he was giving me a ring. But that excitement immediately turned to devastation. His voice was shaky when I picked up the phone. He told me that his father, the father of my 13-year-old daughter, was dead.

I didn't believe him. Maybe I *couldn't* bring myself to believe him at that moment, but I thought it must be a twisted joke. I told him to stop playing games and hung up the phone. But he called me right back, hysterical. He said he was dead and they'd just found him that morning.

That's when it really sank in. This was reality, and there was no escaping it. My life and, more importantly my daughter's life, would never be the same from that point forward.

Adding to the pain was the terrible déjà vu that gripped me. March 3 was the same day I had lost my first, unborn child, fifteen years earlier.

The feeling was overwhelming. I pulled over to the side of the road on Highway 75 and threw up continuously for five straight minutes. How could this be happening? How was I going to go home and tell my daughter that her father was dead, that he'd taken his own life?

It would be the ultimate test of strength and endurance, the two things I had dedicated my life to. By this point, the act of enduring was already hardwired into my DNA. I was, and am, a survivor—of addiction, of abuse, of eating disorders, of losing a child, of being a single mom terrified she'd have enough money to feed her daughter, of starting my own business from scratch and fighting to make it work.

Rod and I had a tumultuous relationship, to say the least. I'm lucky enough to say I've since found the love of my life, but Rod and I were married for eight years. He's the reason I discovered fitness, which is my passion. And he's also the reason I was able to break free of the abusive relationship we had. Still, this was something all the experience and preparation in the world can't help you brace for.

Let me back up.

I'm a high-performance health coach dedicated to helping both men and women live their healthiest life at their ideal weight. I'm also an award-winning fitness bikini competitor, a successful, independent businesswoman, and owner of a local fitness studio and gym.

Endurance is my business. It's my lifeblood.

Endurance is about creating a positive outcome, despite how many obstacles are in your way. It's about turning crap into piles of gold. This is what I preach to my clients—many of whom never enter a race or a competition in their lives. But perseverance goes beyond the gym or the athletic sphere—it's about pushing yourself to win at the game of life. Pushing yourself in the gym past your limits is a microcosm of life, where you're constantly presented with roadblocks that need clearing. Lord knows I've had my fair share.

The endurance mantra was drilled into me from an early age. I was raised by a Marine—and not just a regular Marine, but a high-ranking, lifelong Marine and decorated war veteran.

From an early age, I was taught the importance of grit and resolve. Sometimes those lessons go in a direction you don't expect.

Unfortunately, my unwavering dedication to fitness, at one point, turned toxic.

I was an exercise addict. I eventually developed several eating disorders, including anorexia and bulimia. I was obsessed with being fit. But in an ironic twist, my body started to suffer mightily because of my compulsions.

From the outside, I was an extremely successful, elite fitness studio owner. At the same time, I appeared to be a sleek, sexy, and strong bikini competitor. I had the body our society and culture tells us is a reflection of health and success.

But in reality, I was hiding. I was drowning in a river of shame and deceit. I was disconnected from my truth, afraid and unable to speak my voice.

I know this may sound crazy, but I believed with every fiber of my body that if I didn't look a certain way, I was afraid people would question my authority. The mind is a powerful thing. It's our thoughts that determine our reality. And if you're not careful, it can also rob you of the truth.

Thanks to the lessons I'd learned from enduring previous hardships, though, and an *Aha moment* sparked by my daughter, I was able to overcome my demons. In doing so, I've reached new heights in both my professional and personal life.

Here's how I went to hell and back.

I started my fitness and business journey just as my first marriage was falling apart.

After losing my unborn son, I went down a dark path. The abuse from my husband got worse. It was often verbal and sometimes physical. At the same time, he was abusing alcohol and drugs.

When I first met Rod, he was extremely successful. He was involved with mixed martial arts and also owned a major, multi-million dollar construction company. But as his business took a turn for the worse, his battle with addiction intensified.

I felt like I was suffocating, like I had lost my voice. I felt like I had a weight on my shoulders and that I could never be heard. Fear overcame me.

That started to change when my daughter, Lainee, was born in 2006. My life changed in an instant, and I knew I wanted more for her. I didn't want her to see the struggle and the abuse. She deserved more.

In an odd twist, fitness, the thing that shackled me, set me free—but this wasn't the plan initially. I had actually wanted to become an attorney at the time. Looking back now, more than a decade later, it may seem like it was meant to be all along. But fitness found me, I didn't go looking for it.

Soon after Lainee was born, I started to train. And hard.

I was training to change my body. And the heavier the weights I picked up, the stronger I became physically and emotionally. Because as my body started to change, my confidence increased with it.

Major life changes happened simultaneously. I left my husband about six months after my daughter was born. Then, with my daughter still on my hip, I started my first gym.

Running my own business was exhilarating, but more often than not, it was also overwhelming. I threw myself into making the gym a success, devoting 16-18 hours a day to it.

In those early years, I sometimes worried it was all in vain. Even though I had left an abusive relationship, I felt like I was back to being trapped, trying to find my own way. This time, I was trying to break free of the crippling financial stress I was under. Everything was about the gym. Lainee and I would come to work sometimes at 4 a.m., and she would sleep in the back office while I trained clients. It was so hectic that I would run in, nurse her, and come back out, sometimes with Lainee by my hip, to train another client. Many nights lasted until 10 p.m.

Again, from the outside, things may have looked good to many people. Leaving my husband gave me freedom, and it also allowed me to find my voice. Soon after, I was working to empower other women. I knew I had found my calling. But there was still plenty that people couldn't see from the outside.

One cold and dark December morning stands out in particular. Years later, I can still remember rolling my hands along the carpeted floor of my car, praying to come across some loose change.

All of my money was going right back into my business. It was sink or swim for my gym, and I was trying everything to survive. I was hungry for success. The gym was turning into an elite fitness training studio that was picking up more and more clients. I was still paying every one of my trainers, on top of pumping money back into the business. Meanwhile, Lainee and I were struggling, hard.

I didn't want anyone to know, though. I was embarrassed and in hiding. I felt like an imposter.

Deep down, I worried about not having the education or the knowledge to actually build a successful business. At the time, I was living in my friend's basement, trying to figure things out.

After scrounging around in my car for a few spare nickels and quarters, I took Lainee into a grocery store in Downtown Boise. It was about 5 a.m. when I made it to the milk aisle in the back of the store. My heart dropped. I didn't have enough to buy a gallon of milk.

That was the lowest of the low.

Dejected, I took a seat on the floor in the middle of the aisle and started crying my eyes out with my daughter in my lap. In minutes, she was sobbing hysterically, too. I didn't know where to turn for help or where to go. I was feeling the responsibility of making sure she had a better life than if we had stayed with my ex-husband, and it wasn't going well. So much felt out of my control.

But that's when it hit me. There was one thing I absolutely could control: my body. That's when I decided that, no matter the cost, I would find a way to become the most fit, perfect person in Boise, Idaho. I would compete constantly and win titles because, in my mind, this was the ticket to success.

The plan, as it turned out, ended up working beyond my wildest dreams. But I ended up enduring one major problem, being on the brink of financial collapse, only to create a new, more pernicious issue to overcome.

Soon after committing myself to fitness, it became an obsession, one that was extremely dangerous and almost deadly. The addiction to being fit, and tying my body image to my self-worth, had become my identity.

For nearly a decade straight, I competed nonstop. I was standing on stages at national bikini figure and fitness competition. I was at the top of my game. I was strong and lean, the ideal picture of fitness perfection.

This helped drive more clients into my gym which, suddenly, was a good problem to have. From a business standpoint, things were going great.

Yet the beauty of fitness faded when my health started to suffer.

I developed a deadly addiction that revolved around having a perfect body. This manifested itself in multiple eating disorders. I starve myself during the day, often times only eating lettuce for days on end. I'd do this while working out like a professional athlete. I was burning nutrients that my body didn't have. When I would eat something of substance, I typically ended up forcing myself to throw it back up.

Bulimia is ugly.

After years of falling deeper into my eating problems, I learned how to hide the scars of this abusive relationship I had with myself. I knew how to hide how cold I always felt because I was chronically over-trained and had zero thyroid function. I was running eight miles a day and lifting weights for an hour before doing hot yoga on top of it all. There was never a rest day. I starved my body of rest, and I starved my body of nutrients.

One Christmas Eve during this cycle, I was up late, hanging a few more lights or getting one last gift ready for my daughter. The urge hit me to go into the pantry and have something to eat, but I was weeping.

I tiptoed into the kitchen. I had been fighting so hard to hide my problems from my family that I didn't even grab a spoon, afraid that I'd make a late-night sound. I entered the pantry, still weeping, and grabbed a fresh jar of peanut butter. I sat on the floor and dipped my fingers into the jar while the tears rolled down my face. Tears of sadness, shame and guilt. I was reflecting on the dark dragons I had inside of me. Some call them demons. For me, they're my dragons. We all have them. They're those thoughts, emotions and actions that tear us down time and time again. It's the abusive cycle we create in our mind, a cycle that, for me, ended every time with my finger shoved down my throat. That peanut butter was the only food I had allowed myself to eat in days. And still, I was forcing myself to throw it back up. To this day, the taste of peanut butter makes me tear up. And my mind goes right back to that night on the floor.

From the outset, I was the picture of health. On the inside, I was broken, hurting and exhausted. I hadn't menstruated in more than eight years, and my hormones were completely out of balance. I had developed an autoimmune disease, chronic insomnia, and my thyroid was failing.

If you looked close enough, you could see my hair was falling out.

I was a fitness addict, and I learned that addiction steals from us. It stole my joy and stole precious time I could have spent with my daughter. It hurts to remember, but I missed my daughter's first gymnastics meet because, instead of sitting in the audience, I was literally on a treadmill. My mother sat in the audience instead. Nothing could curb my addiction. I missed events constantly. I never went to dinner parties, because I didn't want to eat.

Somehow, though, I made it through to the other side. But my breakthrough didn't come because my health was on the brink, with my thyroid at an all-time low, my hair falling out by the clips, and going without a period for years. Not the autoimmune disease nor the chronic insomnia were enough to make me change course. It was my daughter.

It's often said that our children will teach us our greatest lessons, and that couldn't be truer for me.

As a single mother, my daughter and I were closer than the average duo. One night at the dinner table, when she was about seven years old, Lainee asked me if I had ever eaten anything other than lettuce.

I broke down, but my action from there led me to break through. I made the decision to sharpen my sword and slay those damn dragons once and for all.

The last 15 years have been remarkably trying, both physically and mentally, but they've also confirmed the old axiom, *What doesn't kill you only makes you stronger.*

I'm stronger now, hardened from the years spent struggling to get my business off the ground and my health in order.

It's been about five years since I pulled through and overcame my eating disorders, and things couldn't be better. Back then, I was convinced that if I wasn't in perfect condition, my business would suffer. Who would listen to me if I wasn't in perfect condition?

I've since learned that perfect isn't aiming for size zero jeans, and that I can eat, exercise an appropriate amount, and still have a thriving business.

Wellness is now a pillar of my life, not the literal moment-to-moment focus. What I stand for, above all else, is endurance. On that, I want to share a few action steps for you to keep in mind, because they've helped me continue to endure the challenges I face on a daily basis.

1. Endurance is the solution for atrophy

Physical endurance is the key to every other kind of endurance. It acts as a conduit between the areas of your life you are effective at enduring and ignites the ones that aren't. But there is a caveat. There are two sides to the endurance coin. The first side is the ability to irrevocably commit to showing up no matter what. It's what David Goggins has been so effective at conveying with a military mindset that resonates deeply with me. "When you think that you're done," he says, "You're only forty percent into what your body's capable of doing. That's just the limit we put on ourselves."

You're already an expert in endurance in a lot of areas of your life. Maybe it's intellectual endurance, where you can stay with a hard situation that needs to be solved until it's done. Maybe it's emotional endurance, where you love someone who seems impossible to love, and you're there for them every day because it matters. And maybe you already know how to endure physically. That kind of endurance equals high performance and impact.

And here's why I say physical endurance is key to all other forms of endurance: When you feel pain—when you're tired and hit the wall—your emotions, your psychology, your mind will tell you to quit. That's the amygdala talking to you, the part of our brain that controls the fight or the flight. It's screaming "Abort! Save yourself!" But to learn to endure physically, you have to flip the script.

As a high-performance health coach, my job is to pull you forward; it's to pull out of your physical comfort zone so you can apply action precisely in the areas of your life where you need it. My clients hate it at first when we find their wall and push them past it. Their amygdala is telling them to stop.

But for authentic growth, we have to go beyond the limits our brains set for ourselves. My clients end up loving it, too. They tell me it pushes them and drives them in virtually every aspect of their life. Because when you train your physical body to endure when you're faced with challenges, your body and your brain know exactly what to do and how far they can actually push past that wall. So you can take yourself further than you ever thought you could go. That's endurance and precisely applied action.

But first and foremost, the foundation on which the Empire is built is unequivocally your health and fitness.

My clients hate it at first.

That's the amygdala talking: Anger, "This might hurt… It might be hard!"

But in the end, they love it. Their prefrontal cortex kicks in, and they make the choice to irrevocably commit fully and happily based on the evidence they've created. Once you learn how to move out of your amygdala and into your executive function. You're in control.

2. Knowledge isn't power

It's not enough to say knowledge is power. I had all the knowledge I needed, but what I really needed was precision. I needed someone to help me take that knowledge and apply it exactly the way I needed in order to make a change.

This is what really counts: Knowledge plus precise action equals high performance and impact. That's true in the gym and in life.

If you're on the keto diet or something similar and it's not working out the way you expected, it's because uniform advice gets uniformly bad results. Here's what I mean: When you chase the fad diets or the newest fitness gimmicks, you presume that because it worked for someone else that it should work for you. Newsflash: you're unique. You have unique needs and requirements, and there is not another genome like yours. It would be irresponsible for me to stay here in this space and tell you that you can do all the same things and get the same results by eating the same thing, working out the same, and thinking the same thoughts. It completely ignores your uniqueness. It ignores science.

Everyone will start at a different place, with a different plan on a journey to the top of the same longevity health-span mountain. I've been on that journey. But just like climbing a mountain, your foot won't land in exactly the same spot as mine. But it will land in the spot that allows you to move forward. If you know where you're going and you know what you need to endure to increase your performance, you can get there. Endurance is a tool, not an outcome.

3. Change the angle to improve the outcome

When you work out and lift weights, your muscles will adapt over time to the stress you're putting them under. They become efficient, but they also stop growing. They stay static as long as you continue to do the same thing over and over again. They can endure because they're used to it. And they can do it for a very long time, but there's no growth.

The secret is to change the angle.

I know the secret to continued growth, in the gym or in life, is to shift the way that you're viewing something. Whatever you've been positively enduring is where you've developed competency, but that's also where you've stopped growing. Your greatest opportunities are where you haven't yet built endurance. The best way to grow is to change your angle.

The problem, however, is that we usually have a hard time seeing those areas where we can grow for ourselves. We need outside support, someone to tell us when the angle has lined up perfectly or when it's completely off its mark. If we don't have that type of coaching and accountability, the worst-case scenario is that we get complacent. Find that person who will change your angle and help you find the spots where you're lacking. That's where real, continued growth comes from.

What I Stand For: Since that terrible day in March, nothing has been the same. How could it?

My ex-husband, Rod, was seemingly getting his life back together. Over the previous five years, he'd started to become a major part of our daughter's life. He made sure he went to her soccer games. He was more present. He started showing up.

And in a blink, he was gone, without warning or explanation.

But even though the pain was gut-wrenching, Lainee and I have still found a way to move forward. The lesson I've learned, whether overcoming severe eating disorders or finding a way to make my business work, even when the money is tight and the odds are long, is that I can endure more than my mind tells me I can. Endurance is the solution for atrophy. That's what I teach my clients and, most importantly, my daughter: Dig deep and push beyond your limits, when life is unbearable.

There's one more thing I want to stress: You can survive even the most harrowing adversity by shifting into a generous mindset. In your time of crisis, look for opportunities to be of service. In my case, everything hasn't magically gotten better in the last year. But by taking what I've learned from my past and trying my best to instill those lessons in my daughter, it's helped both of us to heal.

I was near penniless at one point; a single parent, and battling a debilitating eating disorder. Now I'm running a successful fitness business, making money doing what I love, and living a healthy and happy life. Soul success, to me, is using those bumps and bruises I gained along the way to propel me forward and help others make it through their own challenges.

In the end, I stand for endurance. What will you stand for and what will you stop enduring that isn't serving you?

It's something that creates meaningful change in your life. Getting in alignment with your true core values, going the distance, showing up no matter what, and being irrevocably committed to your vision and mission in life is what it's all about. Period.

It changes your life in the most wonderful, meaningful ways and the result is that you get what you've always wanted.

CHAPTER 14

Trauma

I met Kathryn through a mutual friend. We were both interviewed for an online show about stress. The host of the show saw that we both live in Idaho and decided to make an introduction. "Megan, meet Kathryn. I think you both live near each other."

As it turns out, not only did we both live in Idaho, but we both lived in the same small freakin' town! Not only that, we had about 150 friends in common. Another divine connection. How had we not met yet?

Kathryn is the definition of badass. She has sat with the 1st Lady Michelle Obama, published books, founded non-profits, coached Fortune 500 companies, spoken on large stages, and more. When I first met Kathryn in person, I invited her to a business luncheon I was hosting in town for local female entrepreneurs. At that luncheon she invited us to work with her for a free Brainspotting session. Many of my clients scheduled sessions with her, and what I experienced afterward was incredible! They all seemed so much more relaxed and confident in their work. The excuses diminished, the limiting money conversations disappeared, and their energy shift was magical. It was like Kathryn had lifted the dam of every inner struggle to dissipate and never be seen again. I don't think I had ever experienced such drastic shifts in energy so quickly. Dr. Kathryn Guylay is a woman who knows her shit. She's done it all. And, she has the secret sauce to transform the brain.

Dr. Kathryn Guylay

Six (Surprising) Stages of Soul Success

Stage One: Denial

"Your brain shows what we call a trauma signature."

Trauma. I tried to let the word sink in. My mind (or was it my defensive brain?) screamed in protest and scrambled to build a case against what I was hearing.

I was participating in a post-QEEG (quantitative electroencephalogram) evaluation with a neurofeedback specialist. After struggling with insomnia for over fifteen years, I was desperate for answers. I had tried just about every other avenue one can imagine, so "brain mapping" was somewhat of a last resort. Brain mapping involved having electrodes all over my scalp to read my brain waves to see if there was something out of whack. I was open-minded, but the word "trauma" was one I did not expect to hear.

Trauma does not describe my life experience. How can a suburban working mother have anything in common with a soldier at war or families living through a natural disaster? The voice of Denial had kicked in in full force.

Denial is the first phase of a model described by Swiss-American psychiatrist Elisabeth Kübler-Ross that plots the reaction to any form of personal loss, significant rejection, or tragedy. In my case, I simply believed that my diagnosis was somehow wrong or did not apply.

Kübler-Ross' model starts with Denial and then moves to Anger, Bargaining, Depression, and finally, Acceptance. This chapter is my own story of moving through the stages of Kübler-Ross' model but also building to soul success. It is a story of moving beyond Acceptance. It is a story of using alchemy to turn losses, rejections, and even personal tragedies into nuggets of gold.

My story will demonstrate that we, as soul success women, are capable of going beyond Kübler-Ross' model. We will never stop at Acceptance. We instead move ahead to the Lift-Off stage to Soar to our soul success.

Stage Two: Anger

"You have high beta in your occipital and temporal lobes, particularly on the right side. High beta is associated with anxiety and stress. Even more troubling is a phenomenon we see in your brain called *alpha blocking*. We look for an alpha spike to offset the high beta, but in your brain, it doesn't happen. Alpha should increase when your eyes are closed, but your brain is suppressing these alpha spikes. Your brain always seems to be in hypervigilance, watching for danger."

I was starting to get angry as I listened to this story about my "broken brain."

My brain has gotten me far in life. It got me through a graduate program in international business at the age of 25. My brain catapulted me at age 28 to become the youngest Senior Manager at my management consulting firm. Those three-ish pounds of jelly-like tissue allowed me to grow my consulting unit to 7-figures by age thirty.

I felt my face redden with anger as the neurofeedback specialist continued.

"We see these brain wave patterns in someone who has experienced something that completely overwhelmed their system. Your brain protects you through the survival instinct, so it adapts by amping up in some areas and shutting down in others. You mentioned that your insomnia started after the birth of your second child. Was there anything of significance that happened at this time?"

Ugh. Do we have to get into this? The pathology-obsessed doctor who misdiagnosed my son in utero at 20 weeks with encephalitis? Or when I heard the heart-stopping diagnosis all alone because my husband was at work and wasn't able to attend my appointment? Or was it when the feelings of abandonment skyrocketed during the ensuing three months of bed rest?

I allowed those feelings and memories to arise to the surface.

Why me? It's not fair! Why did no one show up? I had a toddler underfoot and was utterly helpless, unable to stand up without experiencing contractions that were dangerous to my unborn child. I had dozens of relatives in the area, but the help I needed did not show up. I was not a priority. My husband was too busy at work. I had to resort to hiring nearly round-the-clock, hourly help to make sure my toddler did not destroy the house, or herself, during those slow and painful months of bed rest.

Okay, so I had a lot of unresolved anger issues. What was next?

Stage Three: Bargaining, then Depression

"Just do what you can to get the baby to thirty-seven weeks," my OB/gynecologist said as I lay like a beached whale in her office.

I had been marking a big "X" on the calendar for each day that I made it through, one at a time. I had gone from being a kick-ass consultant producing tons of deliverables and value every day to being the person that could barely pen an "X" on a calendar. I had eventually accepted the reality that my working days were temporarily over, and I mourned the loss of my fulfilling and rewarding career. I admitted that I had been a workaholic. I went through the bargaining stage, hoping to avoid a full-out experience of grief by making a deal with the Universe that I would lead a more balanced life if we could just get through this.

The bargain: I have been overly focused on revenue, income, and my bank statement for the past decade. I'm ready to be more in balance. Please, Universe, let me deliver this child healthy, and I promise to be a servant of making this world a better place.

"I thought this day would never come!" I said to my husband as I put an "X" through week 36, day six. I was going to bed, and the morning would dawn with the much-anticipated goal of week 37.

I never made it through the night. My water broke, and our boy was born at 37 weeks, but healthy, thank the Universe.

My C-section incision became infected post-surgery, which required a nuclear bomb's worth of antibiotics. In the years to come, I would experience weak immunity and bouts of bronchitis, sinus infections, pneumonia, and other illnesses. These illnesses were setbacks that kept me from returning to work as quickly and as fully as I had expected.

I became depressed. I didn't sleep. I was alone, as my husband traveled all the time. My mind made up unhealthy stories.

My husband's clients are more important than I am. I never come first. I am not enough. I will never be the top priority.

I continued to float down shit's creek.

Stage Four: Acceptance

"You are a human being, and this was a trauma related to a bulls-eye hit to your emotional vulnerabilities around being abandoned. Your brain reacted to protect you."

A brain that protects me. A brain that remembers the deep pain I felt as a kid when my parents fought and later divorced. The neurofeedback specialist's words had previously not landed, like a cargo plane hovering over a strip in a rural area with geese running everywhere, squawking and flapping their wings in a blurred panic. How could anything land in the middle of all of this mayhem?

The geese were the chaos in my mind. The cargo of the plane consisted of valuable insights I was unable to receive while my mind remained a noisy and messy place. The ideas, the gifts of intuition and Acceptance, didn't connect at first. Once the geese cleared, the plane had a place for a clean landing. I was ready to accept what had happened in my life.

I turned to positive psychology. I found the work of Martin Seligman, Shawn Achor, and Marci Shimoff. Shimoff has famously explained: "Rejection is God's protection."

I began to address the negative dialogue in my head in a positive way:

I had to suffer through bed rest. *Yay! Someone or something finally made me slow down.* I had to give up my brilliant career and the big paycheck. *Phew! That path was about to be my worst nightmare, sucking all my time away from my life's mission and passion for helping others in a new and creative way.*

I'm sick all the time and have a broken brain. *Yee-haw! Figure out how to optimize yourself so you can optimize others. Study and master brain-based healing modalities and natural medicine. Be a guinea pig for your healing methods and techniques; you go, girl!*

I face abandonment issues. *Rock on! This inner and outer work is going to come together like an amazing and beautiful puzzle. Your struggles can allow you to create a career and life filled with purpose and passion. You can help others deal with similar issues to what you've faced with more grace and ease.*

As soul success women, we accept our losses, rejections, or tragic events with openness. We study them as dedicated students of classroom Earth. We glean lessons from our failures, embracing the words of author and speaker Robin Sharma.

"There are no mistakes in life, only lessons. There is no such thing as a negative experience, only opportunities to grow, learn, and advance along the road of self-mastery."

Self-mastery starts with clearing the geese off the runway so the cargo plane full of insight and Acceptance can land. Clearing the geese is possible through contemplative practices such as yoga, mindfulness, and meditation. I'll talk more about these practices in the tips section at the end of this chapter.

Stage Five: Lift-Off

"It would be difficult to sleep with this brain," the neurofeedback report concluded.

Yep. Not easy to sleep with night sweats, either. I can't believe I've spent thousands of dollars on organic mattresses and sheets, temperature-regulating sleep pads, EMF-regulating devices, black-out curtains, and white noise devices. I've ended up feeling like Princess and the Pea, but awake!

I went on to learn that there were many other variables involved. I learned that my genetics predisposed me to sleep issues, detoxification challenges, and hormonal imbalances. If I remained in Denial, Anger, Bargaining, Depression, or the endpoint of Acceptance in Kübler-Ross' model, I likely would have never improved.

As soul success women, Acceptance is just the beginning of our transformation—we Lift-Off. We create affirmative action and traction in our lives. We find our next level of evolution and growth. To do so, we are flexible and open to change. We consider the advice of many transformational experts, including one of my favorites, the 900-year old Jedi, Yoda: "If no mistake have you made, yet losing you are ... a different game you should play."

The operative words are "different" and "play." As soul success women, we embrace opportunities to change up the recipe in our businesses and lives. We playfully change directions, finding more fun in life.

The lift-off from my beached-whale mama-broken-brain experience involved the creation of a whole new brand: Make Everything Fun.

I recognized that, as I picked up the pieces of my life and started to put them together, I wanted to have a more integrated experience. I had been living in a world of dichotomies: work/play, coach/friend, consultant/mother, and professional/humanitarian. Switching back and forth between these roles and keeping them in balance was exhausting!

I was also attempting to integrate creativity with wellness and business. I had multiple courses, books, and podcasts that hinged on Fun: Make Leadership Fun, Make Wellness Fun, Make Nutrition Fun, and Make Publishing Fun. I was also running a nonprofit called Nurture.

Could I do all of these things in a more integrated way? As a soul success woman, the answer is *Yes*. I unified my projects under Make Everything Fun to consolidate energy to maximize productivity and fullness of life.

How does fun allow us to integrate our lives better? Fun is the fuel that enables us to sustain our efforts when obstacles inevitably arise. To be clear, I am not a Pollyanna who believes that life is all about dancing through the fields of roses. That, as you already know, has not been my experience. Instead, I recognize that life is about challenges that bring about growth and development. This challenging-yet-rewarding road is one traveled by individuals, teams, organizations, and Fortune 500 companies.

Scott Belsky, CPO at Adobe and author of *The Messy Middle: Finding Your Way Through the Hardest and Most Crucial Part of Any Bold Venture,* says that "Curiosity is the fuel you need to play the long game." My spin on the subject is: *"Fun is the fuel you need to play the long game."* Fun *provides a renewable energy source* to survive what can often seem like a Herculean effort to maintain the many long-term projects we undertake in life to learn the lessons assigned to us in classroom Earth.

Stage Six: Soar

"Your mess is your message."

I attribute these words to transformational leadership expert Lisa Nichols, but this was also the ultimate takeaway from my session with the neurofeedback specialist who diagnosed me with trauma.

My mess? A brain that needed fixing, genes that required customized interventions, and a career that required reinvention.

My message? Trauma is part of the human experience. We should never have any stigma or fear around getting help to go through our lessons and crises. Through support, we can do much more than just accept our rejections, losses, and lessons. Together as soul success women, we can lift off and soar!

My process of lifting off and soaring was not simple or easy. It involved integrating inner work and outer work and required creativity and patience. My inner work continued with yoga, mindfulness, and meditation. Having quite a lot of uproar (oh, those noisy geese!) in my mind, I integrated technologies such as photobiomodulation and transcranial alternating current stimulation (TACS) to help me rebuild the alpha and quiet the high beta in my brain. I became certified in modalities such as Brainspotting and Quantum Neuro Reset Therapy that recognized the power of addressing the subconscious in the healing process. I earned a Ph.D. in Natural Medicine that incorporated neurofeedback, biofeedback, and nervous system regulating processes such as Neuro-Linguistic Programming. I became certified as an Epigenetics coach and executive coach. I gained faculty status at the Wellness Council of America. I remained humbled by the complexity that is the human system and retained a belief that no guru or healer has the power to make us whole. We hold the keys to unlock our own human optimization.

Today I work as a coach and consultant applying a complex systems approach to human performance and optimization. I incorporate genetics, epigenetics, cutting edge brain-body modalities, and a humble reverence for each client I serve. I am daily in awe of the complexity of human systems, be they inside of a complex organizational structure or a single human being. I view each system as a work of art.

Themes that remain stable in my life are positive psychology, finding purpose in life, and creating a living legacy. My mission is to inspire and empower individuals and organizations to execute their highest purpose in the context of productivity and fun.

Some of the lessons I'd love to summarize for you are:

1. Clear the geese and chaos from your mind. The Universe can't deliver its amazing cargo of insights if you don't clear that runway for landing. If you're like me and find mindfulness and meditation challenging, seek out professional help to incorporate techniques and technology that can assist you in optimizing your brain-body system.

2. Be open to change. As you begin to tap into the power
   of your subconscious mind, notice what comes up,
   even if it is not comfortable. Seek help if you feel that
   "trauma" might be surfacing, and know that you are
   not alone. One of my favorite experts on trauma,
   Dr. Gabor Maté, defines trauma as a "disconnection
   from the self." Ditch the stigma around "trauma"
   and instead view your inner work as a quest to align
   yourself with your highest, most authentic self.
3. Incorporate some fun on life's journey. As you change
   things up, remember that life is not linear. Nor
   does it always feel like a dance through tulips! Find
   what's fun for you and use that fun as fuel to make
   it through life's ups and downs. As I've mentioned in
   the previous two tips, reach out to others, and seek
   help and support. Have fun together.

We inevitably go through the stages of the Kübler-Ross'
model of denial, anger, bargaining, depression, and acceptance
as we experience rejection and loss. Soul success women move
beyond acceptance to lift off and soar. I have gleaned these
lessons from my own life and from transformational experts
I study.

I'd like to leave you with both a concept from a rockstar
woman author and a quote from the 900-year old Jedi I have
previously mentioned.

The rockstar author is a friend I met when she was giving
a tour for her first book, *Carry on Warrior.* Glennon Doyle
Melton has written about how life is both beautiful and brutal,
a word she combines as "brutiful." When we understand the
"brutiful" nature of life, we are perhaps able to move more

gracefully through the challenging and roller-coaster-like stages of soul success.

Soul success woman, may you go forward on your "brutiful" life journey with more ease and flow remembering the words of 900-year old Jedi I quote to conclude:

"Luminous beings are we."

PILLAR 5

Service and Entrepreneurship

*"Success is not to be pursued, it's to be attracted by
the person you become."*
— Jim Rohn

I like to say that I came out of the womb as an entrepreneur. From as early as I can remember, I was always trying to get people to buy shit from me. I did the lemonade stand thing, went door-to-door selling cookies, and even discovered a hot glue gun! Wow, did buying that glue gun open up a whole new world of possibilities for me. My friends and I would go to the craft store, buy fake flowers and wreaths, and then go to town on our creations. After we were done with our masterpieces, we would put on our rollerblades, tie pillows to our butts, and rollerblade door to door in my neighborhood selling wreaths. I loved the power and creativity unleashed within me, and who could say no to two little girls innocently selling makeshift wreaths?

Unfortunately, when my confidence started going south, so did my passion for entrepreneurship. I no longer felt inspired to create. In my mind, my ideas were stupid.

But after discovering personal development and finding my mentor, my mojo returned. I regained confidence and, most importantly, found myself in the process. I realized that entrepreneurship requires more than just selling. It requires more than a brilliant idea or a great strategy. It even requires more than unwavering passion. The biggest lesson I learned is to work harder on myself than anything else. Becoming a successful entrepreneur means that your personal development and quest for growth never ends. You never stop being the student. Entrepreneurship is not just about business. It's about the person you become.

CHAPTER 15

Creating a Life by Design

I met Kathy a few years ago after she applied to speak at our first Soul Success Summit. We met on Zoom so I could learn more about her story and message. My first impression was that she was beautiful, well spoken, and incredibly smart. I was also impressed with her resume: Kathy holds an MBA, took 2nd place in The Pitch, is a contributor to HuffPost & Vogue, sits on the Forbes Coaches Council, and works with many Fortune 500 companies. This woman is on top! I told myself.

But as she started getting into her story, my jaw hit the floor. I was not expecting her to share so much darkness and, quite frankly, so much contrast from what I read on her resume. A common misconception is that we see successful women and imagine they were born that way. Kathy has experienced immense heartache and darkness, but the key is that she has been able to channel those experiences into massive success. Selfishly, I couldn't wait to get into her head and learn her secrets to shifting the course of her life. I knew our audience would love her.

Kathy embodies radical transformation. When she spoke at the Summit, we were blown away. You'll have to read on to learn about her story, but let's just say it's not for the faint of heart. Her journey is dark and emotional, and horrific—to think that a little girl and young woman could be faced with so much trauma. It's women like Kathy who inspire me to the point of complete body chills. It's women like Kathy who give me permission to play big and step into the leader I know I can be. When we got feedback from our event, almost every single person listed Kathy's story as one of the most impactful parts of the Summit.

It's hard to find Kathy because she's always in a different part of the world when I check up on her. When I asked if she would contribute to this book, she was traveling in Africa and was under strict deadlines. I gave her another deadline. I told her she had less than two weeks to submit her manuscript and, fortunately, she was a yes, because I couldn't wait to share her secrets to massive transformation with you. Her story gives me faith that no matter what situation you might find yourself in, if you use the right tools, you can always find a way to the top.

Kathy Haan

As a child, I always knew I'd find success. I had big dreams and plans to be an actress, and spent my days and nights entertaining my family and friends. I was harboring a secret, though. A secret that brought me enormous shame and guilt. As far back as I can remember, until the summer going into the 5th grade, I was molested by a close family member living in our house. As a young girl, this was very confusing to me. I was afraid to say anything to my parents because this was someone I love and I didn't want them to get into trouble. For a long time, I'd convince myself it didn't happen. But it did happen. It happened like clockwork. Every weekend or so while everyone was in bed, I'd be subjected to his perversion. Sometimes it would happen during the day, too. He'd place me on all fours in the closet while he stuffed pillows all around me so I couldn't see what was happening. These incidents are some of my earliest memories.

It stopped when my mother got a job in Oregon the summer I went into 5th grade. We moved halfway across the country, and that family member stayed behind in Minnesota. My childhood was mostly happy, filled with lots of swimming, camping, road trips, and food. Oh, the food.

I was a fat kid. I distinctly remember the first time I turned down a donut because I knew I was too fat. I also remember stepping on the scale, seeing it go over 100 pounds, and restricting my eating until it went under 100 again.

Unbeknownst to me, my mother had passed on her eating disorder through comments about my weight and what I ate. This continued into adulthood. My mother came to my first child's baptism when my daughter was two months old. And in her presence, I reached for a few peanut M&M's set out on the table of my mother-in-law's house. "You'll never lose your baby weight if you eat those," she warned.

As a pre-teen and teen, I was sneaking snacks to avoid any confrontation with her. After my mother and stepfather were in bed, I'd line my pockets with granola bars, fruit snacks, and trail mix. I'd fill a great big mug with milk and cereal in case I was caught on the way back to my room—I'd tell them I was only getting a drink of water. Then I would eat—all of it. When finished, I'd take a shower and make myself throw up all of the food into my mug. I'd shower, and then empty the contents of my stomach into the toilet bowl and flush it.

When my mother discovered a graveyard of wrappers under my mattress, she put a lock on the cupboards. I knew where the key was, though, and I would still sneak food. When caught again, I was grounded from eating treats or snacks for the entire summer. At my own birthday party, I sat and watched all of my friends eat my birthday cake, ice cream, and snacks.

As you can imagine, this sort of thing completely wrecked my relationship with food and my body. Throughout high school, I binged and I purged. I cycled through periods of orthorexia nervosa and anorexia nervosa. My weight fluctuated significantly throughout these years, and still does.

When I was 14, my mom was married to her third husband. We lived in a huge house on the side of Mt. Tabor with perfect views of Mt. Hood and Mt. St. Helens. In our driveway sat two Mercedes, a Karmann Ghia; in the garage, a Porsche. We had a 44' sailboat down at the yacht club. And in our own house, I wasn't allowed upstairs. They had motion detector alarms that would tell them if I went upstairs, although they kept it locked. It was their part of the house.

I knew where that key was, too. And one day while they were at work, I went upstairs and into my mother's closet. Her closet contained the only scale in the house, so I grabbed it to weigh myself on the upstairs' bathroom floor. When I was done, I put the scale back, went downstairs, and locked the door again.

That night, my mother and stepfather were up fighting most of the night. I didn't know what they were fighting about until my stepfather barged into my room in the middle of the night to tell me I was no longer welcome in their house. Behind him, my mother stood there in her nightgown, crying.

I stayed with friends for several weeks until I had a plane ticket to visit my elderly father in Iowa for spring break. I moved in with him, where we lived in a trailer just outside of a town of 1,200 people. I distinctly recall hearing him cry over his checkbook at night, trying to figure out how he was going to put food on the table or pay for medications he literally could not live without.

In high school, I led two very different lives. On one hand, I was the responsible daughter who cared for her elderly, disabled father. I worked two jobs—one at the nursing home, and one at Dairy Queen. All the while, I was a cheerleader, VP of Luther League, in the choir, and participated in speech competitions and pageants. On the other hand, I was promiscuous, fond of drinking, and later got involved in drugs—weed, coke, meth. I used drugs as a coping mechanism for the very busy life I led. I felt like I was in control.

As soon as I turned eighteen, just after graduating high school, I went to D.C. for what I thought was my big modeling and acting break. Instead, I found myself a victim of sex trafficking. The clients who saw me were successful men—many of whom worked for the Pentagon and the White House. I couldn't call them out in a lineup now, and didn't care about politics then, so I had no idea what roles they served. I also can't really blame them—they thought they were hiring an escort.

After confiding in one of the clients who took the time to get to know me, he told me he'd help me out. He put me in touch with a Madame who said she could get me out, but that I'd have to work for her as an escort for a few days. I agreed, and in a short period of time, I was back home in Iowa. My college roommate told me she'd get me a job at her work as a stripper. At that point, I was so detached from myself and my body that I agreed to that, too.

One night while working at the strip club, a twenty-something year old came in and whispered in my ear, "*Katherine?*" I was taken aback because we all used stage names instead of our real names. As it turns out, this was someone I'd been speaking with on Yahoo Messenger. We hung out every day, and after about a month and a half, I hadn't gotten my period in a while. I took several pregnancy tests, and they were all negative. I was relieved, because we were both using cigarettes, meth, and coke pretty heavily.

On January 7, 2005, I took another pregnancy test in the Walmart bathroom. I sat there for fifteen minutes before realizing I was reading the wrong side of the test. I flipped it over and was horrified to see it read positive. I walked out of the bathroom trembling and nodded to my boyfriend that I was pregnant. I threw out the pack of cigarettes and vowed to never touch drugs ever again.

I spent my entire pregnancy terrified that my child would be handicapped because I used drugs before I knew I was pregnant with her. She came a week before my 19th birthday, and she is perfect. To this day, she's the best thing that ever happened to me. If I didn't end up pregnant, I'm sure I'd be dead or in prison by now.

When she was born, her father moved in. We got along for the most part, although he had a habit of making me feel stupid and being a little rougher than I'd like. One night, with my infant daughter on my hip, her father punched me in the face during an argument.

It wasn't until after we were married and had another child that I realized I was in an abusive marriage. When

I wasn't sleeping, I was crying. I had crippling anxiety and missed work for three to six months at a time. A psychiatrist diagnosed me as bipolar, and I was put on a lot of medication. I went to an intensive outpatient group therapy for four hours a day, four days a week. It was there that I finally built the courage to tell my husband I was leaving him.

At first, he was incredulous. His emotions cycled between anger, sorrow, and then something I recognized as manipulation and gaslighting. He was brilliant but manipulative. He got into my head and convinced me that because of my depression and alleged bipolar condition, I'd never see my kids again if I left him.

I believed him. I believed with every fiber of my being that my children were better off without me. I was a burden. They didn't deserve to have a mom like me. I had put them through far too much. Who needs a mom who just sleeps and cries?

The details that follow are a bit fuzzy as I was so heavily medicated. From what I remember, I had tucked the kids into bed and then went into my bedroom and I took my entire bottle of prescription sleeping pills and downed it with a glass of water.

The next thing I knew, my husband was dialing 911, and my two-year-old was running up the stairs to my father, sobbing and screaming, "Mommy Die! Mommy die! Mommy die!"

The last thing I remember that night was feeling deep regret. What had I done? How could I have done this to my kids? My father? My God. What had I done?

As the stretcher carried me to the ambulance, I called out, "I'm sorry. I'm so so so sorry,"

When I awoke, I was in the ICU with all kinds of cords and wires strapped to me.

My father was sitting next to me, sobbing. He had given me a hug and told me he was sorry. Apparently, my sister had told him the source of the sexual abuse I had endured my entire childhood, and he felt immense guilt from not being able to protect me.

I spent the next nine days in the hospital. While I was there, I saw a child psychiatrist who recognized my mental illness for what it is: PTSD, from the trauma I endured as a child. I was not bipolar. No wonder my medication wasn't working. I left my husband when I got home, and a few months later, I was medication-free.

After a nasty divorce and custody battle, I met a man who inspired me to be a better person. Together, we worked out every day, started a coaching business, and married on our one-year dating anniversary. I've since been to 28 countries. I write this on my laptop from the Kenyan Maasai Mara, where I have the pleasure of documenting a scientific expedition for my blog.

People ask, what was the catalyst to my radical change? And I've got to say that what might look like an overnight success is never really that. It's 5,527 days of resisting temptation. It's 3,223 days of focusing on my mindset and health versus allowing life to just happen right in front of my eyes. It's about creating a life by *design* rather than a life by default, because I sincerely feel that the secret to telling a great story is Living one.

I was *never* the smartest or the brightest person in the room, but I had passion, I had grit, I had conviction, and I knew that I could outwork anyone else to create consistent results in my business. Had I not gone through all of the trauma, the adversity, the addiction, the abuse—I would not be where I am today. I would fold if I were told *no*, or face even minor resistance.

Some of you here might be facing some of the challenges I did, back when I couldn't get out of bed, when I felt like it was everyone else's fault, and that the world was out to get me. I was jaded because of the trauma that I went through. I was angry that everyone labeled me and told my story for me.

If this is you, know that you're not alone. You are worthy. You are valued. You are loved. You have so much to give back to this world, no matter your trauma, no matter your scars, no matter your burdens. You may carry an enormous weight and you may not have a white knight to save you. Sometimes, we've got to be the ones to save ourselves.

There's a lesson one of my many mentors taught me, and it's this:

Life and its trauma are not happening TO YOU, it's happening FOR YOU.

If I hadn't hit rock bottom that night as they wheeled me out on a stretcher after overdosing, I wouldn't be sharing my story with you today. Know that for a really, really long time I hid these stories in the back of my closet like secrets until I realized that strategy served no one.

Brené Brown says that if we can share our story with someone who responds with empathy and respect, then shame cannot survive. I found my silver lining, and that's helping women create a life by design so that they don't have to go through what I went through.

Now, I've got a mission for you: Find your silver lining and reject the story you're given. Tell *your* story unapologetically, because there is someone out there that needs to hear it.

I'm a firm believer that the secret to telling a great story is living one. I spent years miserable, suicidal, and unable to leave the house because of crippling anxiety. I was miserable because I was in a constant state of victimhood. Sure, really shitty things happened to me. I had to decide that no one else was going to come to my rescue—I had to do it myself.

Many people think that having success means you've arrived. I disagree. True soul success is so much more than that—it's a journey—one that's meant to be embraced no matter how bumpy the ride. Your soul is on a path toward the horizon. Like an actual horizon, you're never going to reach it, but, oh, look at that view!

Each of our journeys may look different. Some may be blazing new trails, conquering tremendous feats, and living so loud that people are left in awe in our wake.

Others prefer a quieter trek, marked with calm waters, wind in their sails, and the sun on their backs. No matter what your journey looks like, you know you're on the right path when you wake up excited for the day. If you're miserable and dreading your job, don't be afraid to let go of it. If you died tomorrow, they'd replace you the next day. Your dreams and your goals are worth fighting for. If not now, when?

Kathy's Three Activities for Soul Success

1. Embrace your multiple passions. There's a message in the coaching world that you "haven't arrived" if you're making money doing things *other than just coaching*. What a load of bullshit. Start that coaching business, do freelance writing for magazines, make money blogging, set up a social media marketing agency, and create a publishing company—all at the

same time! If you genuinely love the work you do, you'll work a lot but you're going to enjoy the hell out of it.

2. Pivot. When I first started my health and fitness coaching business, I did so because I lost 123 lbs. I started blogging my journey, and the blog gained a lot of traction. Brands started sending me free stuff to review, and before I knew it, I had a table full of gadgets and gizmos to review. So, I started charging for writing about brands on my blog. Then, people were amazed that I made money blogging and wanted to know how to do that, too. Over time I realized I don't really like working out or eating healthy, so I pivoted. I focused on helping women launch and scale coaching businesses, which then led to me making really great money. I started doing significant international travel, and realized I wanted to write exclusively about travel on my blog. I still help women create online businesses, travel blog, and do a few other things.

3. Create a personal brand. I'm talking to you—network marketers! Don't let your network marketing company be the face of your business. If you decide to pivot as I did, then having a personal brand will allow you to do it in near-seamless fashion. But if you're sharing about four different network marketing companies you're part of in any given month, you'll lose credibility with your audience. Building a personal brand allows you to showcase your talents, passions, and life in a way that doesn't make people think you're flaky.

4. Involve the family. Some of you may not work very well with your spouse, so if this is you, ignore this message. However, if you're feeling the strain of long hours away from family, involve them in your work. Instead of hiring out to a freelancer, look at what tasks you have in your business that can be done by your own family. For example, my daughters love helping me write blog posts. My son, with blond curly hair that old ladies love to touch, loves to pose for pictures for my blog. He has sensory processing disorder, so having both of his parents home and in business together has helped him immensely.

CHAPTER 16

Adhd, Perfectionism, and Monkey Brain Math

Who doesn't love a Rose? Rose Jubb is upbeat, vibrant, and uber successful. I met Rose through a mutual friend and we became fast friends. She's confident, well-spoken, fun, and absolutely gorgeous. I was so happy she agreed to speak at The Soul Success Summit for not just one, but two back-to-back years because she's on fire, baby!

When she came on stage for her first speaking appearance, she wore a hot pink jumpsuit. For real. She was literally glowing on stage. I needed sunglasses not just for her jumpsuit, but her teeth. I mean, who has teeth that white, straight, and perfect? Rose. Besides being bright and fun, she is also wicked smart and successful. She is an in-demand speaker, podcast host, author, and host of her own television show on Amazon Prime, *Closet Goals*.

When I started watching her show, I realized how much work I needed to do on my own wardrobe and physical space. De-cluttering is such an essential step to transformation and leadership. I realized that many of my blocks were not just in my mind, but also catalyzed by my physical space. Rose gives us the tools to de-clutter and find confidence in the way we look and feel. In this chapter, you're going to hear a more personal side to Rose, one that she doesn't normally talk about to her audience. She explores the deep-seated doubt and attachment to perfectionism that most entrepreneurs face when launching.

So ladies, get ready to stop and smell the Rose. Roses make us feel sexy and this Rose is no exception. I invite you to get ready to step into the sexiest, most confident, and fun version of you there is. Again, I'm pointing right at you, babe.

Rose Jubb

Being a Wardrobe Stylist can seem so glamorous from the outside. The clothing, the events, the photoshoots. It is impactful, creative, challenging work, especially when I get to help women really *see* the woman they are and will be in the mirror. I do this through DIY video style courses and private programs for clients who are able, but also teach gals tips through a podcast and even a makeover TV show called "Closet Goals."

Transformation is powerful, and as long as it is an up-leveled version of that person's real personality, it can imbue clients with so much natural confidence and propel them toward their goals. But wardrobe styling *is* still a business, and even the most glamorous businesses require paperclips, paying taxes, and picking up the phone to sell something. You may have started reading this thinking, "Cool! A stylist! She'll talk about style for success or trends." Sorry to burst your bubble. Today I'm going to talk to you about entrepreneurship and mental wellness, specifically identifying and letting go of old beliefs that could be holding your business back. It's something I call Monkey Brain Math which reaches way back to our cavepeople cousins, back before walk-in closets, when animal print was almost your only option on date night.

As a wardrobe stylist, I often get put into a few buckets that I actually have nothing to do with. People sometimes assume I'll be catty, or obsessed with labels, or shallow. If I'm networking and the room finds out that I'm a stylist, two things usually happen: 1) Almost everyone I speak to apologizes to me for what they are wearing, which triggers the same mom-joke from me every time, "Oh, I don't judge anyone until they pay me," before I give them a teasing wink and ask them about their goals. Or 2) They want to align with me somehow through making fun of what everyone else is wearing. They quickly find out I'm not into that. There are few exceptions to this rule, however, and I have found that the bigger the players in the room, the more likely they don't feel intimidated by my industry. They know there is ROI in looking and feeling their best.

It was at one of these events, with a room full of women I admired, that I learned a huge lesson about my old beliefs that were sabotaging new business.

The Big Reveal

There I was, in a hotel ballroom with 200 powerhouse women business owners, getting up out of our uncomfortable chairs. I'm a wardrobe stylist, so my job at conferences like these is to basically show up, look fly, expand my mind, and get leads. All was going to plan until we were broken into small groups for an exercise, and I was asked a question about sales jitters, and then I suddenly cried in public!

Yikes!

What just happened? What on earth turned on the tears at this conference in front of these strangers? Well, a very kind business coach happened to call me on a few things. But in the best way possible.

You see, I had just asked this small group how I could ease the nervous feeling I had before sales calls that seemed to be getting worse with every win.

You read that right.

I had just launched a new private client, year-long, styling program and something just clicked with this product! It's like I finally asked the right questions and put together the right package. AND BAM! 100% close rate, baby!

Prospective client after prospective client said yes to the program on each call. But instead of my nervousness about the sales calls diminishing with every win, it only increased. The evidence was telling me they would probably say yes, but my stomach was telling me, "Your survival depends on not picking up that phone."

I know now that this is my brain trying to keep me small to keep me safe. Not reaching out avoids social risk, which could lead to getting kicked out of our village. Getting kicked out of the village means death. So, socially awkward moments equal possible death.

That's what I call Monkey Brain Math.

Every time I was getting ready for a sales call I'd listen to a bunch of lady rock, I'd get brave, I'd pick up the phone, and close another new client, only to get even more nervous for the next call.

When I explained this odd problem to the group of women I was standing in at our conference, some teased about what a fantastic problem it was. Some told me to try to "enjoy the process instead of focusing on the outcome." But one business coach just gently said, "Why is 100% so important to you?"

Me: What?

Her: Why is it so important to you to close every call? You keep repeating 100%.

Me: Well, the business certainly is better when I do. *chuckle*

Her: Yes, but your stomach is telling you to fear the call intensely despite repeated evidence that sales calls are easy and even fun for you. Do you think that keeping that 100% might be *so* important to you that you dread calls beforehand because logically you will *eventually* have someone say "NO"?

Me: *tears fly from my eyes*

Her: What was school like for you?

For context, I have training in mental health and social science, which put me in the classroom with some pretty amazing professors who were also therapists. I have also spent time on both sides of the therapy room, but this gal's ninja skills were beyond!

It was suddenly so damn clear.

Dazed, Distracted, Dumb

Throughout my childhood, school was tricky. I was constantly losing time, popping back into my head after daydreaming for who knows how long, only after a teacher called my name multiple times. I couldn't pay attention, doodled constantly, was so upset when someone figured out I read as slow as I did, and really took to heart being in the slower groups for everything academic.

Getting teased at school, on the bus, and even at camp about being distracted, losing things constantly, and not being able to stay organized sent a very distinct message to me: I was probably just dumb.

We aren't born with a roadmap or instructions, so sometimes we just get told something we don't know isn't true and hold onto it, because it happens to be one of our first self-descriptors. I struggled to keep my grades just below average in high school, and the only thing that pulled my GPA up was the fact that I could ace any art-related class and could usually talk teachers that weren't in the Art Department into creative projects (e.g., I once made a diorama as a book report).

English class was difficult because as hard as I tried, the information didn't sink in. To this day, I still couldn't tell you what an adverb is. This sentence is probably incorrect in some way. And this one probably is too.

Math and science were interesting, but I'd show up to class excited to learn, then look up from a page full of doodles fifty minutes later and class was over.

In high school, there is a huge yearning to sort yourself into a group, but I didn't really fit into any. I wasn't a cheerleader type, wasn't in the chess club, wasn't on the newspaper, didn't realize I had musical talent until after college, wasn't coordinated enough to be considered a jock, wasn't a partier, had braces, and was taller than every boy until senior year. It was *greeeaaaaat.*

I promise you this late bloomer was a serious wallflower. In fact, I spent a lot of time literally painting flowers on walls. When I couldn't even pay attention in the class, or pull more than a C average, you can imagine how I'd just learn to lean toward those art classes and assume that that was all I could do.

After high school I applied to one college, a local technical school that taught graphic design. That was probably all I'd be good at, anyway. I mean, I loved the transformative power of clothes and would have loved to be a stylist, but I assumed you had to be ordained by the editor of VOGUE or something to do that. That wouldn't happen to just any dummy from the middle of Minnesota. So, I simply kept that little dream under my hat.

But the funniest thing happened in graphic design school: I landed myself on the Dean's List every semester!

It was AMAZING. Every class I attended: stats, psychology—all A's! Even English. I can hear you shifting in your seat, wanting to yell, "Rose! You had an attention deficit disorder and needed to study something you love to be able to focus!"

And you would be right. Gold star! My confidence skyrocketed in college. Which was wonderful and needed. But because I was looking for something to identify with, I quickly stepped right into "The Queen of the Dean's List" role. And that brand of perfectionism is damn lonely.

I continued living up to this role through my Bachelors in Psychology and my Masters in Social Science.

Slowly but surely, I began to attach my value to my performance of being at 100%. This followed me through my marketing career, becoming a counselor, and even when I pivoted to personal styling after having my son.

This "100% performance = my value as a human" belief followed me all the way to a Women in Business conference where it promptly showed itself, manifesting in running mascara and a stunned look on my face.

What I couldn't see until then is that I was not only *actually* nervous about *not* getting 100%, but I was also nervous that I'd slip back to that lost feeling that came with not performing well, feeling dumb, lost, and worthless to my village.

So what's wrong with perfectionism rearing its head like this? I mean, I was still closing every call. Crack out the tiny violins.

The problem was my fear of failing (translate: anything less than 100%) was keeping me from stretching. It was keeping me from raising my prices. It was keeping me from reaching for bigger clients. It was keeping me from following up with people I wasn't 100% sure would say yes. It was keeping me from calling, and in fact, it made me require clients to actually chase *me*.

Do you know how many clients I probably have left behind because I thought they might not say *yes*? Think how my services could have positively impacted their confidence and business. *I* stole their chance for having that positive result from my services by simply not asking them if they were interested.

Don't join me in this. Don't steal your talents and gifts from the world. Don't make the assumptions that we all instantly make about people (how much money they have, their education, etc.) rule whether or not you push yourself past your own limiting beliefs and offer them your services.

It's Just a Question. Not a Tiger

You may identify with this fear of inviting new clients into your business, too. First, you should know something about fear and anxiety. They are built-in security systems meant to keep you safe. There's a problem, though: As humans, our circumstances have changed faster than our circuitry.

We're still walking around with parts of our brains that are not as advanced. We're wired for social groups because we were safer in social groups before we had weapons, houses, locks, police, hospitals, or TV shows about survival. If being left alone in the world means death—which is exactly what our Monkey Brain tells us—then we would do everything in our power to avoid losing our value in the group.

That was exactly my escalating sales call problem.

My Monkey Brain Math (limiting belief) was that perfect equaled value. If that's true, then not continuing to close 100% of the time would mean I'm not perfect, and not valued, and not needed by the village. Hello, tigers! Goodbye, safety!

How have I overcome this?

I've had to devote time and effort to accepting what I have to offer the world has a real positive impact. Seeing the full value of it and being proud of what I do has helped me reframe the sales process from Asking to Inviting.

No more, "Please get this service from me, because of these reasons." More of, "If this is a good fit for both of us, I'll invite you to bet on yourself in this new way."

Before learning how to do this, my business completely relied on people coming to me with their needs, people buying courses quietly and anonymously, and the random client here or there that would find a booking link and sign-up themselves.

I've also written my mission down and can see it multiple places while in my office. I have a shortened version that I can quickly say when talking to people about my business. This keeps me tapped into why I do all of this. My discomfort in the moment of a *no* is worth it if I can reach my goals of getting on the biggest stage possible to spread as much confidence and self-love as possible to women and girls around the world.

I may never cure cancer, but if I stay brave and remind myself that my Monkey Brain Math is flawed, I just might help a woman grow the confidence needed to go for that promotion, run for office, or apply for that research grant. Confidence in propelling bold women toward their goals is my positive ripple.

To me, that's real success. Getting paid to make a positive impact on the world, doing something I was born to do.

Now, my earnings have tripled. I'm on my way to my first six-figure year as a one-person business, and I just keep growing as I put more effort into getting in front of the right women who see the value of looking and feeling their best, and make invitations to them actively if I feel they would benefit. It's their job to say *no* if they don't want the services I have to offer.

Not to mention, I get a new pair of shoes for every 20th *NO* I get.

Rose's Activities for Soul Success

1. If you think you struggle with a possible learning disability or attention issue, don't feel alone. So many successful entrepreneurs do. Our brains are

wonderfully different, and often have the ability to hyper-focus on the things we're passionate about. I spoke to my doctor when my brain was just too noisy in my 30's after having my son, and I learned I have ADHD, which makes sense looking back. Medication has helped me tremendously, but there are so many other treatments and tools to employ.

2. If you're good at something that could make a positive impact on someone's life, Do Not steal their opportunity to grow! Invite them in and leave it up to them whether or not they'd like to take advantage of the opportunity. Coming from that angle of service to them and the world has calmed my sales call anxiety tremendously.

3. Repeat after me: "Perfectionism is not a positive character trait. Perfectionism is a curse."

If you let it, perfectionism can hide your talents and gifts from the world forever. Waiting until something is perfect to present it to the world doesn't work because nothing is perfect for everyone. Use the energy you would have used to make things "perfect" towards getting your message out and your business will be better off.

CHAPTER 17

My Time in Jail

After the 3rd grade, I had completely given my power away and lost all confidence that I could create magic. I let friends and boyfriends influence my decisions. I got into trouble because of it. I partied my little tush off because alcohol was the drug that brought out my inner-child superpowers. A couple shots of tequila reminded me that the little girl who danced in her tutu, the same girl who wanted to start a school newspaper, was still in there, and she was fun!

But eventually I realized that although she was fun, alcohol was not a reliable friend, and she sure as hell wasn't there to bail me out of jail after I got my DUI. Not alcohol, and not my girlfriends who were with me when it happened. As a girl who is severely claustrophobic, I can remember those seventeen hours in a tight jail cell so perfectly. I was stuck in a cage with women who were high on meth and cocaine, and my only friend in that cell was a young teenager (another claustrophobe) who got arrested for petty theft. The two of us banged on the gate relentlessly, hoping someone outside would hear us and come to our rescue. We so desperately awaited someone to help set us free. When someone finally did come hours later, they told us to fuck off. We had given our freedom away.

There was a pay phone in that cell. I stared at it relentlessly wondering who was going to be my phone call to pick me up. Not my parents. Please. It would break their hearts. I would be their one disappointment and prove to them that my sisters were all angels and I was the fuck-up in the family. So I called my girlfriend. She was my friend who was with me the night before. She had taken off her seatbelt and stood up in the car. After I told her countless times to stay seated, she stood up to dance and change the radio station. She was why the cops pulled me over and discovered I had been drinking. I was trying to give her and our friends a safe ride home and she fucked it up. I thought she must have felt awful and was waiting for my phone call. So I called her. This was back in the day when we actually remembered our friends' phone numbers.

"Hey Meg! You okay?" She picked up the phone.

"Sort of. Can you pick me up? I'll be out in a few hours?"

"Hmmm... I'm at a BBQ. Just call your dad."

My heart sank. My "friend" couldn't leave her damn BBQ to pick me up from jail? The next few hours sitting in that cage led me to reflect on how I got myself into that damn cell anyway. I realized how much faith and trust I had put into people who didn't deserve it or really even want it. I had spent the first ten or so hours mad at my friends for putting me there. It took me some time to realize how wrong I was, to realize that *I* had put myself in that cell. *I* made the decision to drink that night. *I* made the decision to drive my friends home.

It was in that cell that I realized that I had spent the past twelve years blaming others for my circumstances. I had spent all those years letting other people take my power away. It wasn't my girlfriends who got me the DUI, it was me. It was always me.

The same week, I got fired from the corporate job I hated and broke up with the boyfriend I disliked. I was lost, alone, broke, and confused. It was time to take radical responsibility and change my life.

Shortly after my DUI, I discovered personal development. I started attending workshops, listening to CD's. (I'm not certain if podcasts or YouTube were even a thing yet). I became certified as a personal trainer and began studying yoga and meditation. The worst thing that could have happened to me ended up being one of the best things that happened to me, because it woke me the fuck up.

They say that before expansion comes contraction. In order to build and get stronger, a muscle needs to break down a little bit. I was broken in that jail cell, and it was all my doing. Not my friends, not my boyfriend, and not my 3rd grade teacher. It was all me. I had defined myself by how I thought others thought of me. I had put myself in a box. But there was still work I needed to do. Even though I realized I had dug myself into a deep hole, I knew I was meant for more. I was nowhere close to being the person I knew I could become. It was time for expansion.

I thought that the answer to becoming the best version of me meant that I had to go back to school. I so badly wanted to become an agent of change, so I applied to several schools for my Master's Degree and got into my first choice, USC. This was my vehicle to become the advocate for kids and their ideas. I would tell them to go write that school newspaper if they wanted to! I was thrilled to be on course to make a difference.

On my first day of grad school, my professor praised the world of counseling. "Most of you will leave here with a full-time job before you graduate. Nothing can ever replace your job and your gifts. I guarantee you are secure."

Sweeeeet! I thought. I was going to get a good job before I even graduated. I was no longer going to be broke. Sure, I wasn't going to be rich, but at least I could pay the bills and that was enough.

Two years later, 2008 happened. California laid off 30,000 teachers and counselors. There were zero counseling opportunities in the schools. Zero. I was worse off than before, because now I was six figures in debt and still had no job. Six months of sending applications out to schools who might one day need a counselor and not one freakin' interview. When you're in school you can live off of student loans. But after you graduate, they actually want you to start paying for it. Not only was I unemployed at that point, but my student loan money—the rent money—stopped coming. And I was more than $100,000 in debt.

I tried to go back to cocktailing, I tried to go back to personal training, I tried everything. Each time I tried I would see little income, but never enough to pay the bills. Not nearly enough to pay my landlord $1,200 in rent.

So I got creative.

I started selling textbooks on eBay, got small gigs here and there, but I still needed to make more money. Then one day as I was leaving my apartment, I ran into my neighbor who was walking with a kid from Germany.

"Meet my exchange student from Germany!" she said.

"Nice to meet you! How long are you here?"

"Oh, about two months."

"Awesome, how did you guys meet?"

"Oh, so many young adults want to come live in Los Angeles. There is a foreign exchange program that is desperate for nice American families to take in these kids, and they will pay you good money for it."

Eureka! I thought.

God bless America.

Two hours later and I had convinced my roommate that we were going to be the "nice American family" to host foreign exchange students. Even though we were in our early twenties, couldn't pay the bills (or groceries) for that matter, and could barely take care of ourselves, we were going to adopt foreigners.

Brilliant.

My roommate, Cynthia, was in med school and could use the money, too, so she liked the idea, even if it meant us sharing my bed for a few months while strangers slept in her room.

They say that desperate circumstances force creativity. Somehow, I managed to stay in that West LA apartment for one more year. I honestly don't know how I came up with money, other than foreign exchange students, random cocktail gigs, and selling shit on eBay. Eventually, I had exhausted my resources and was forced out of my apartment.

Then one day, while all this was happening, I received a phone call.

It was a woman named Heather. She was calling about a health coaching opportunity.

I sort of knew what she was talking about. I had applied for a hundred jobs and sales opportunities on craigslist. I applied for things I would never apply for, and this was probably one of them. There was a part of me that wanted to hang up on her, but then there was another part of me that knew that if I wanted my circumstances to change, then I would need to shift my perspective.

"Is this Megan?" she said.

She sounded like an old friend. I could tell by her vibe that she was someone I wanted to hang out with. She told me about their office in Culver City and invited me to come check it out. Even though I was a bit resistant, there was something inside of me nudging me to meet her.

A few days later, I drove over to the office to meet her and the team. The office was hard to find so I had to circle the block a few times before seeing a handsome man with a clipboard standing outside.

Fuck. It was one of *those* things.

This was going to be one of those cheesy, learn how to become a millionaire seminars located in a sketchy back alley. I didn't even have my pepper spray. I was about to leave, but there was a voice inside my head begging me to stop my car and get out.

You'll never know what lies ahead of you unless you take a leap of faith. That voice went on. And besides, sister, it's not like you have any other options right now, so get your broke ass out of that car.

I got out of the car and walked into the office located in the sketchy back alley. When I walked up the stairs I was greeted with young, friendly, and good-looking men and women. They were all so eager to meet me and learn about me.

If you know anything about Los Angeles, you know strangers are not friendly. If they are, it means that they want something from you. What did these people want from me?

I stayed there for an hour and met everyone in the room. I heard story after story. They were stories like my own. These were people just like me. Some of them had masters' degrees and some even held doctorates. Some were ex-pro athletes. Some had just gotten laid off from corporate. The one common theme with all of these people was that they were fed up with other people making decisions for them and decided to make something of themselves. Some of them were making pretty good money, but that's not what stood out to me. It was the community that stood out to me. It reminded me of my days as a competitive athlete. I was intrigued.

Since I was a personal trainer, working with nutritional supplements seemed to be a smart source of revenue. I knew people who wanted to get healthy and now I could actually help them without having to actually train them. But I still had no idea what I was doing, so I knew that if I wanted to be successful, I would need guidance.

When Heather greeted me that day, I wanted to be her. She was confident, charismatic, and an excellent public speaker. Several of her clients were there that day in the room. For an hour I heard story after story, how she had changed their lives. She was a person of impact. It was at that moment that I realized that if I wanted to be successful, I would need a mentor. Heather was it.

For the next year, I walked into that office every day and sat next to her. I listened to her phone calls, her daily routine. I paid attention to the way she spoke to people and praised them. Then when I would have a sales call scheduled, she would sit next to me and listen. She believed in me. She believed I could accomplish things before I believed it myself. Even though I didn't fully believe in myself, I believed in her ability to coach me. I believed she would change my life, but I would need to *let* her. I would need to be open and think outside of the box.

That first month, with pure desperation and inspiration, I made $1,200. That was enough to get by. I couldn't believe it: $1,200 at that time was a lot of money to me and the exact amount of money to pay rent, but it still wasn't enough and Heather knew I was made for more.

"You're going to hit $10,000 in sales this month," she said.

It was my third month in business. I had no idea what the hell I was doing and I didn't even understand what $10k meant. Ten thousand dollars might not sound like that much money to you, but I was broker than broke.

"Show me how you can create $10k," Heather said. "Map it out."

She said it again. And again.

Little did I understand, but Heather was coaching me on some of the key principles to manifestation. You have to believe in it so much that it's real before it's actually created. You've got to tap into the emotion of what it will feel like receiving the $10k, to the point of zero resistance. Every day that month we talked about $10k. I woke up thinking $10k. I wrote in my journal. $10k. $10k. $10k. $10k.

I looked at the people in my life who would help make it possible. I wrote down their names as if the $10k already happened, and I celebrated it as if it had already happened.

Most people get it backwards. They wait for things to shift before they believe. Manifestation doesn't work that way. You have to believe it and see it out first. At that point, I believed, with every cell in my body, that it was going to happen because in my mind, it already had.

When I finally hit $10k that month, I knew that it was the beginning of a new chapter for me. No longer was I going to wait for things to happen. No longer was I going to wait for others to decide my fate. It was all up to me. I stopped submitting resumes for counseling gigs, I stopped applying for jobs, because I had big things to do. The world needed me in new ways now and I was about to manifest a new life beyond compare. This was the beginning of me stepping into the leader and entrepreneur I was meant to be.

I am grateful every day that Heather introduced me to the world of entrepreneurship and helped me start my first business.

To think that was me, eleven years ago, turning piles of shit into nuggets of gold. I stepped into a deep pile of shit but through alchemy, I was able to turn it into something beautiful. I have coached thousands of people since that first encounter with Heather. I have helped my clients achieve the impossible, from losing 100+ pounds to making $100,000+ dollars a year. I have helped my clients retire from Corporate America, build global brands, become in-demand speakers, authors, philanthropists, and changemakers. I have opened studios, sold out programs, and created events where women actually want to fly in from other countries to attend. I have spoken in front of thousands of people. That little girl in a tutu would be proud.

I say this not to toot my own horn, but to give you permission to step up and become the leader you've always wanted to be. You've heard some pretty badass stories, and my wish for you is that you take this book as your permission to go baby, go! I've got my Pom Poms in my hand right now and a sign with your name on it. I'm your biggest fan. I believe in you.

So now I'd like to leave you with my 5-part framework that can help you in any situation you might find yourself where you're knee deep in the shit. After countless years of studying transformation, coaching my clients on transformation, and living in transformation, I have created 5 simple steps to alchemy: turning shit into gold. This framework is based on the same principles that have been around for thousands of years. It has been inspired by mentors like Abraham Hicks, Ram Dass, Gabby Bernstein, Dr. Joe Dispensa, and some of the women you just read about in this book. My request is that with anything you learn, you customize this framework in a way that works for you.

Your 5 Step Framework to turn shit into gold

1. Identify: In step one you must identify the trauma, wound, obstacles, and limitations. Become hyper-aware of the emotions you are channeling today that are not serving you. Most people live their lives a victim to their emotions, but not you. You are not reactive, you are proactive. Becoming proactive means that you must understand where you give your power and attention. Recognize the people and the things you focus on and how they affect you.

   We don't know where we put our energy until we start to understand the triggers that pull us off course. For two decades, I didn't realize how much power I was giving to other people. I had to identify the conversation that was holding me back from manifesting what I wanted. In telling myself that my ideas were stupid, I was subconsciously looking to prove that statement true.

If you're unsure what your limiting beliefs are, the first step starts with setting a big goal. If you knew you could achieve it, what is one big desire that you would pursue today? Then, write down every excuse, limitation, and objection you have for why you won't achieve it. Great questions to ask yourself: *How do you really feel about your desire? What is getting in the way of creation? Did something happen to make you believe that you are unable to achieve what you want?*

2. Clear: In step 2 we gain the tools to clear the space of negative emotions and energy. Absence of negative thoughts stops the momentum. In order to rewrite the story, we need to clear the space so that the negative patterns stop taking power.

Sometimes it can feel impossible to be positive when we are so deep down the rabbit hole of negativity. When my kids are screaming at the top of their lungs and relentlessly punching each other in the face, it's hard to see them as my "sweet little angels." And to be honest, I'm just trying my best not to lose my shit and scream back, so finding joy in that moment is just not realistic. I'm not the Buddha! However, finding tools for you to clear the space and create an absence of thought is much more doable. In that situation, this is what I can do: I can walk away from them for a minute. I can close my eyes. I can focus on my breath.

Clearing the space requires you to access the tools to shift your focus away from the rabbit hole of stinkin' thinkin'. This is a powerful resource, love.

Meditation is something you can do anywhere, at any time, but maybe sitting and breathing isn't your jam. Find another form of meditation from things that bring you joy (e.g., walking, reading, listening to music, writing, lighting a candle, surfing, skiing). The important thing is that you have your toolkit ready to access when you need it.

3. Declare: In step 3 we create a mantra or list of empowering statements that propel your mission forward. This mantra aligns with your desires and empowers you to shift your energy towards co-creation. A great way to develop these statements starts by looking at all the excuses we wrote in step 1. Next to each statement we write an empowering statement to contradict the limiting belief. For example, if your limitation is "I don't have enough experience and there is no proof this will work," you can counter that statement by saying something like, "I am ready and willing to take the necessary steps to achieve success. I am resilient and ready to do whatever it takes until it manifests."

You can also break down the statement into a simple, one-word mantra. When I realized I was living a life of scarcity, abundance became my mantra. Everything I did was "Abundance." I woke and the first word I said to myself was "abundance." I would eat abundance, breathe abundance, sleep abundance. I would visualize abundant creation every day. When it came to money, I would write big numbers and tap into the feeling of receiving that amount of money. I would write checks to myself in the amount I was manifesting. When it came to impact, I would go into rooms and visualize hundreds of people sitting there as students of mine. I would make the decision to feel abundance in my breath, my blood, and my bones.

I would tap into the feeling of things that were already abundant in my life such as love, relationships, adventure, and opportunity. I would relish in that feeling so that abundance and I would become one. I would then imagine that exact feeling affecting other areas in my life, especially money, as that was my biggest area for growth and expansion. I would imagine my bank account growing. I would imagine clients writing me checks. I would imagine my organizational sales numbers increasing by the day.

4. Awareness: In Step 4 we turn on your emotional thermometer. How you feel about everything is Everything. Become hyper-sensitive to your thoughts and emotions. Ask yourself *How can I access joy from this?"* Create a plan to access your toolkit when things do not feel good. Tune into your mantra or empowering statements and provide evidence that supports you.

A prime example of this is getting a "no" on a sales conversation from a potential customer. When we hear no, often we translate it to things like, "My service is not valuable," or "I am not worthy of their money." We begin to develop lies about ourselves that have nothing at all to do with their decision. They likely said *no* for a completely different reason (e.g., they didn't have the money, they aren't mentally ready to make an investment just yet). Women do this a lot. We make the *No*'s about us, even though the reasons often have nothing to do with us, but about what is going on in that other person's life.

Find an empowering statement that will take power over the lies you tell yourself in situations like these. Then develop your truth. For example, the truth is "I have an incredible service that has resulted in hundreds of lives transformed. I am a master at my craft and have produced results like (x). The person said no because they have too many wheels spinning in their life. They just weren't ready."

5. Manifest: The final step requires you to get really good at accessing the joy around everything you do. Understand that this is a choice rather than a circumstance. Instead of being reactive, become proactive and attract what you desire using the laws of attraction. Build the momentum for prosperity. If we want to become magnetic manifestors, we must look at manifesting the same way Olympic athletes treat their sport. Just like they practice daily, we too must practice the laws of manifestation daily. Repetition is the key to mastery.

Conclusion

Making the decision to stop reacting to other people and their wants, and taking the reins of my life, has shifted everything. It wasn't easy at first, and quite frankly, there are still days I look in the mirror, and say to myself, "WTF are you doing? Girl, you are crazy!" But the big difference is that I bounce back. I realize that all the voices in my head telling me I'm not enough are bullshit. Before, I made the choice to allow scarcity to run my life without even knowing it. Now I tell scarcity to go take a hike because abundance and I are in a committed relationship. Yep, we're soulmates.

When I first became an entrepreneur, it seemed like everyone around me was waiting for me to fail so that I could go back to my "real job" and finally find "security." The people around me loved me; they wanted me to have a comfortable life. I get it. No one wants to see their loved one struggling to make ends meet. No one wants to see all the money they invested in their degrees to go to waste.

But I had a vision. I was ready to enter the arena.

Did you know that the #1 regret most people have when they are dying is listening to the people around them instead of their intuition? In other words, when people look back on their lives with a clear mind, they realize that many of the big decisions they made were to please others instead of themselves and their own fulfillment. Most people die feeling like they had not honored their own dreams.

Can you truly say that you are honoring yours right now?

The reality here is that it is not an easy path, which is why most people die feeling this regret. It's hard to start a business or become a leader. It's hard to create something out of nothing. It's hard to get uncomfortable. But when you make a decision to enter the arena it will be much harder to look back on your deathbed wishing you had listened to your voice.

> *"A miracle is a shift in perception. The moment*
> *that we chose to perceive our life with love,*
> *we can create a miraculous change"*
> — Gabby Bernstein

When you enter the arena, there are times you will be tested. Many years ago I was broke, lonely, and unfulfilled. But there was something inside of me that knew the pain of not following my dreams would far outweigh the pain of acting on them. So wherever you are in your business or life goals, I need you to understand that I feel your pain. I understand your discomfort. It might be easy to fall into the idea that you need to follow the path others want vs. your own dreams, or to land a comfortable job because it will be better for you.

I call bullshit.

The feeling of victory knowing you followed your intuition is one of the juiciest feelings one can experience. Yes, it can be messy, but that's the beauty of it.

When I made the decision to launch Soul Success®, it was ugly. No one cared about my ideas. For months, no one bought tickets to our first event. But then I realized that I made a commitment. I had already declared my dream and now I was trying to go back on it? Hell no! I made the decision that it had to work, and I was going to figure out how. I am grateful every day that I didn't give up. I wouldn't know most of the women in this book had I given up. I wouldn't have the clients or the community that I have today. I made the choice to pursue my dreams even though it wasn't always pretty. I got uncomfortable, and what kept me going was my unwavering faith in the mission. I took a stand and I've never looked back. Had I given up, you wouldn't have the book in your hands right now.

Imagine the lives you will change when you act and take a stand. Never give up.

Now it's your turn. Go turn heads, babe. Your life depends on it.

Thank You's

Behind every strong woman is a tribe. Sara Connell, you were an angel from heaven. I could not have completed this project without your love, support, and guidance. Thank you for believing in this project and giving me the tools to bring my dream to life.

Melissa Pharr, my business guide and believer in all things possible. Thank you for your patience and keeping me in check throughout all my crazy ideas. Heather Schwartz for becoming my first mentor and stretching me to a new level of possibilities, co-creating our lives together.

To all of the authors in this book: Kathy, Rose, Pirie, Jenn, Jaya, Jaime, Leah, Jamie, Sara, Jesse, Barbara, and Kathryn. Words cannot express my gratitude for being a yes. It is divine energy that brought us together to bring this message forward. Thank you for clearing time out of your lives to make this a priority and submitting your memoir in such a short deadline. It speaks volumes of you who are.

Thank you to my friends and family for all your support. Mom and Dad, I couldn't have picked more generous, thoughtful, and loving parents. I must've done something pretty cool in a past life to win you as parents. It is the biggest honor to be your daughter. To my sisters who always loved and celebrated me. To my in-laws who treat me as your own daughter. I love you all.

And lastly, to my husband Luc and two girls Mykala and Galena. You three are my WHY, my everything. I do this for you. Thank you for molding me in the wife, mother, and person I am. I couldn't be happier or more honored to be with you every day. I love you more than words could begin to express, my loves.

Author, Megan McCann

Megan McCann is a Business Strategy Coach & the Founder of Soul Success®, a global personal development and leadership brand designed for female leaders ready to reach their next level. She holds a Bachelors in Sociology, Masters in Counseling, 200 hr Registered Yoga Teacher, and in 2011 made it to the top 2% of a multi-billion dollar nutrition company.

She currently works with entrepreneurs, philanthropists, intuitive healers, speakers, authors, and other creatives, and give them the tools to scale their business, more specifically, increase their value, make more money with less effort, and tools to find alignment in their life and business.

Megan has opened yoga and nutrition centers and studios along the West Coast. Her global events, retreats, business summits, mastermind, 1:1 coaching, and online tools give current and future change-makers the tools to harness their highest potential. She lives in Hailey, ID with her two daughters Mykala and Galena, and her husband Luc.

To apply to work with Megan please email support@ meganmccannyoga.com or visit TheSoulSuccess.com

TheSoulSuccess.com
MeganMcCannYoga.com
IG: @themeganmccann, @thesoulsuccess
Find Megan McCann and Soul Success on Facebook

Contributing Authors

Sara Connell

Sara Connell is an author and founder of Thought Leader Academy where she helps coaches, writers and entrepreneurs make a massive impact by becoming successful, published, bestselling authors and in-demand speakers. She has been featured on The Oprah Winfrey Show, Good Morning America, The View, FOX Chicago, NPR, and Katie Couric. She has presented to a wide range of organizations from Fortune 500 Companies to local and national organizations such as: Avon, Estee Lauder- Origins, Johnson & Johnson, Jones Lang LaSalle, GE, Northwestern & Northwestern-Prentice Hospital for Women, Unilever & the Young President's Organization. Her writing has appeared in: The New York Times, Forbes, Good Housekeeping, Parenting, Tri-Quarterly, IO Literary Journal, Schlock, Psychobabble and Evolving Your Spirit. Her first book Bringing In Finn was nominated for ELLE magazine Book of the Year.

You can find her at www.saraconnell.com

Jamie Green

Jamie Green is an Empowerment Activator, Energy & Embodiment Coach and Entrepreneur. She co-creates healing with conscious individuals to enliven the light we all hold in our hearts. She inspires inner union with our Divine Feminine and Masculine through the wisdom of our sovereignty, and the whole embodied expression of our unique Essence.

More info at jamiegreenhealing.com

Pirie Grossman

Pirie Jones Grossman is a certified Life Coach, TedX Speaker, writer and producer of wellness festivals around the country. She has shared the stage with speakers such as Deepak Chopra, Kris Carr, and Jill Bolte Taylor. She leads women's empowerment workshops, including teenage girls, focusing on self esteem, sleep disorders, depression and brain health.

She's a former TV host for E! Entertainment Television, Fox Television, NBC, CBS and ABC. She was Co-Chair for the Special Olympics International World Winter Games in Idaho and spoke at the UN on behalf of Special Olympics.

She is the founder of the "Love is Louder" Brain Health Summit with Suicide survivor, Kevin Hines, focusing on teenage depression and suicide. She also gave a TedX talk about, "How To Heal A Community from Suicide."

Pirie has her Masters in Spiritual Psychology from the University of Santa Monica, California. She is a Sun Valley Wellness Institute Board member. She is a co-founder of the Own Your Throne podcast with Diane Chandler. She lives in Sun Valley, Idaho with her two teenagers where she has a private Life Empowerment coaching practice.

More info at www.piriejonesgrossman.com

Dr. Kathryn Guylay

Dr. Kathryn Guylay is an agent of change serving transformational organizations and individuals. She combines best practices from a management consulting background with coaching skills and tools for highly effective communication, strategy development, personal branding, and marketing. Kathryn has an MBA and Ph.D. in natural medicine with a focus on brain-body wellness. Kathryn's expertise has been featured throughout many events and media, including ABC, CBS, NPR and hundreds of radio interviews and articles. She has published six books and hosts two podcasts, syndicated across all the major platforms. She is known for being "relentlessly helpful" to her clients. Kathryn loves delivering speeches and workshops on topics spanning positive psychology, leadership, communication, holistic wellness, and creativity.

More info at www.makeeverythingfun.com

Kathy Haan

Kathy Haan believes that the secret to telling a great story is living one. As a result, since 2010 she is an international speaker, author, business coach, top travel blogger, and influencer; Kathy works with some of the largest brands in the world. She took 2nd place in The Pitch, was a contributing writer for the Huffington Post, and a Forbes Coaches Council and Vogue Influencer Network member.

In 2020, she took home the Be a SHERO Foundation's SHERO of the Year award and was the victress and honoree of their annual red-carpet gala held in Las Vegas. You can find her in places like Forbes, USA Today, Reader's Digest, PARADE, and Parent's Magazine.

Kathy helps women all around the world create online businesses far bigger than their dreams; helping them to realize their fullest potential. She is founder of the Turning Coaches Into Millionaires Radio Show, Bucket List Adventures, a Certified Law of Attraction Practitioner and

Reiki Master. Kathy lives in Iowa with her husband, three children, and two Great Pyrenees.

More info at https://www.idyllicpursuit.com

Jesse Johnson

Jesse Johnson is a master sales and success coach, specializing in helping spiritual entrepreneurs build 7-figure businesses. After 12 years of teaching math in NYC public schools, frustrated by bureaucracy, she founded her own personal development company and built it to 7 figures in just 2 years. Jesse now teaches sales as a spiritual practice - no compromise, no self-sacrifice, no mediocrity.

More info at www.jessejohnsoncoaching.com

Rose Jubb

Rose Jubb is an image consultant, TV style expert, and visibility coach who not only works with personal clients both in-person and online, but also developed an entire platform called Style Class. This platform helps women dial in their style and personal branding from the comfort of their homes. Her book 'Closet Goals', podcast 'The Boss Closet', and course 'The Boss Closet Makeover' are now complemented by her makeover show 'Closet Goals' available on Amazon Prime Video.

Along with her experience in style and design, Rose also worked in marketing for many years, studied psychology, and has her Masters in Social Science. This extensive background helps her guide her clients towards presenting an image that attracts exactly what they want from the world while being completely themselves.

More info at www.mystyleclass.com

Barbara Kamba Nyathi

Barbara is an author, inspirational speaker, lifestyle coach and social psychologist. She is also an entrepreneur with a flair for the finer things in life.

In 2015, Barbara was a finalist in the Namibian Economist Businesswoman of the Year, and in 2017 she received an award for inspiring women and was also recognized as one of the most influential women in Namibia. In 2019 she was awarded the Confidente Woman of the Year award in Namibia. She is the Zimbabwean and Namibian country head for First Class On Your Becoming — a sisterhood established in honor and celebration of women.

She is passionate about empowering women and transforming their lives.

More info at www.bolddialogue.co.zw

Jennifer Ludington

Jennifer Ludington is a high-performance health coach with 15 years of experience coaching and training high performers, athletes, high achieving professionals, CEO's and entrepreneurs. She believes that living your life at your ideal healthiest weight is the number one business, leadership and personal relationship key to success in life. Jennifer is a wife and mother, former elite fitness studio owner, fitness model, yoga studio owner, National Level Fitness and Bikini competitor, endurance athlete, speaker and founded and later sold a nutrition bar company FitFuel, LLC designed for high achieving professionals.

Jennifer owned and operated a premier elite training facility in Boise Idaho for over 12 years where she guided and taught the leading trainers in her area as well as opened additional locations, a yoga studio and pitched and sold her protein bars to Albertsons and Natural Grocers.

Jennifer has a unique take on the fitness industry after suffering in silence for over 8 years ridden with shame and guilt of massive eating disorders that affected her health in order to keep up with the social media unattainable images in the media. She believes that health is not always what the fitness and diet industry dishes out and is committed to bringing true health and wellness to an industry obsessed with external fitness perfectionism.

More info at www.jenniferludington.com

Jaime Rivetts

Jaime Rivetts MS Ed is the Executive Director and founder of Idaho Social Learning Center. ISLC was founded in 2012 and Jaime has been in private practice helping families understand the social world for the past 15 years. Jaime is deeply passionate about helping children and families find their place in the social world. No child should feel left out or alone and struggle to make friends. Jaime runs weekly social learning groups in a variety of different schools, after school groups at her clinic, and individual sessions to dive deeper into a child's needs. She also contributes to a variety articles online, runs a Facebook support group, and is currently working on a children's book series. Jaime is the mother of two adorable little girls and understands the challenges of being a parent. You can find more information about Jaime's programs at jaimerivetts.com

Jaya Rose

Jaya Rose is the creator of She Rise Global. An online brand that helps empower women to own their power, speak their truth and create a ripple effect of positive change, through entrepreneurship. She lives in Portland Or, with her husband, youngest daughter and Charlie the Goldendoodle + Chance the cat.

More info at thejayarose.com

Leah Warshawski

Leah Warshawski produces features, television, commercials, and branded entertainment around the world. Her career in film began in Hawaii working in the Marine Department for LOST and HAWAII. Her first feature film, FINDING HILLYWOOD (2013) won 6 awards and screened at 65 festivals around the world. Leah's most recent feature documentary BIG SONIA (2017), profiles her 94-year old grandmother (and Holocaust survivor) who still drives herself to work every day. BIG SONIA won 22 awards at more than 75 film festivals and was eligible for an Academy Award. In 2017, Leah gave a TEDx talk entitled "How Do You Cope With the Trauma You Didn't Experience?" She also advises filmmakers on social impact, outreach, marketing, festival strategy and hybrid distribution plans. In addition, Leah co-founded rwandafilm.org in 2012, a LinkedIn for Rwandan filmmakers supported by Bpeace and The Academy of Motion Pictures. This year, Leah earned an Executive for Social Impact Strategy certificate from UPenn. More info at www.inflatablefilm.com